One Fry Short

A Journey Toward Self Discovery and Emotional Success

Compliments of ...
WWJC Radio 850 AM
www.wwjc.com

Tim Passmore

9607 State Road 70 E.
Bradenton, FL 34202

One Fry Short:
A Journey Toward Self Discovery and Emotional Success
by Tim Passmore

Published by Outcome Publishing
9607 State Road 70 East
Bradenton, Florida 34202
www.outcomepublishing.com

First Edition

Printed in the United States of America

1. Religion: Spirituality General
2. Self-Help: Spiritual
3. Religion: Christian Life – Personal Growth

Dedication

This book is dedicated to my wife, Jennifer, who has put up with me for so long. Thank you for being patient as I have traveled on my own journey of self discovery. You're awesome!

Table of Contents

Introduction

Has anyone ever told you you're crazy? One of my favorite sayings about someone who's not completely with it is "he's one fry short of a happy meal." As a parent of four kids, the happy meal reference really resonates. I have a confession to make. I'm a fry short. Well, to tell the truth, I'm more than a fry short. Throughout my life, I've had emotional issues that have greatly affected me. I'm not alone! I've learned that all of us have "issues." Let me put it this way: we're all at least one fry short. We need to be aware of our struggles, know how they affect us, and do what is necessary to control them rather than be controlled by them.

Some who are stressed by emotional difficulties want to give up. Don't! With God, there is always hope. He is with us and wants to help us navigate our lives. The information you'll read in this book will guide you as you look inside yourself and to God's Word to learn His perspective of who you are and who He wants you to be.

What is written on the following pages is really personal to me. You'll read about my journey toward self-discovery. More importantly, you'll learn what God has to say about our emotions and how we can change our thinking to become healthy. My desire is for this book to become personal to you. Ask God right now to help you take a true look at who you are and for His strength to make changes that will lead to a more meaningful and successful life. Let the journey begin!

Chapter One

An Open Book

Therefore confess your sins to each other and pray
for each other so that you may be healed....

James 5:16

The year was 1985 and there I was, sitting with my "hot"
girlfriend, Jennifer, in my red Dodge Charger in a parking
lot at Samford University. Much had happened leading up
to this moment. My first encounter with her occurred when
we were just toddlers. Both of our fathers were pastors in
the Tampa area at that time. Occasionally, the association
of churches would have meetings and our parents would
lug us along and stick us in the nursery together. Although
I obviously don't remember these first connections, I'm
sure she caught my eye. Well, maybe not. A four-year-old
checking out a two-year-old gives cradle robbing a whole
new meaning.

Years passed and we found ourselves in a new city. Both
of our fathers had accepted pastorates in Pensacola, Florida.
The next meeting between us would occur when I was
sixteen and she was fourteen. It was set up by my brother-in-
law who had accepted a position to be the minister of music
in their church. Youth hay rides were a big hit in those days,

so he planned one and asked me to come play my guitar and sing. And who was there? Jennifer! I tell everyone she was star-struck by my musical abilities, but the truth is, I couldn't keep my eyes off her. This would be the beginning of a great relationship over the next eight months.

Things changed when her family moved once again, this time to Spring Hill, Florida—just north of Tampa. Long-distance relationships are hard and ours, like many others, didn't survive. Why, you ask? My "scummy" behavior ended it! She wanted to keep things going and would regularly write, but I wouldn't return her letters. I know, typical male behavior, right?

While we were dating, she and I had talked about the future and our plans to attend Samford. It was part of the love story. You know, go to college together, get married, make a lot of money, and have kids. Pretty big plans for a ninth grader (her) who was dating an eleventh grader (me). Her moving out of the area and my refusal to communicate put an end to those dreams. At least that's what I thought.

Birmingham

I graduated from high school, kept true to my plan, and headed to Birmingham. Two years passed and I began wondering if she would do the same. My fraternity, Sigma Chi, was hosting a party for new freshman students. I turned around and there she was. I couldn't believe it! The spark came back immediately. At least it did for me. Both of us were dating other people. My girlfriend had just graduated from Samford, and her boyfriend was attending another university in Atlanta. We began seeing more and more of each other. She broke up with her guy friend and I would eventually break up with the girl I was dating. The relationship had begun again.

How about another "scum Tim" story? Jennifer thought I'd stopped seeing the other girl when we began to date. Not so! I'd go out early in the evening with her and would hook up with the other girl later on. Jennifer didn't know about this until a fellow fraternity brother, my roommate, "outed" me. I was a little mad. In fact, I was really mad because my fun life had just taken a very bad turn. This caused her, for some reason, to have a problem with me. Can you believe it? She responded by dating other guys. Who would blame her, right? It drove me crazy!

A turning point happened one day as I was having a conversation with my little brother in the fraternity. I'd been assigned to help him become accustomed to fraternity life. He knew Jennifer and I had been dating, but he had no idea what had happened between us. Thinking we were still together, he made a statement to me. He'd become very frustrated over his own relationships and said, "Tim, you're so lucky to have someone as awesome as Jennifer." He was right and I saw the light! Everything became very clear to me at that moment. I blew the best thing that could have happened to me. Realizing this, I immediately ended things with the other girl and began to pursue Jennifer with great dedication and enthusiasm. Fortunately, it worked and she took me back.

The relationship began to grow and trust was being restored. The more we dated, the more I realized how much I loved her and how much she loved me. We were very "real" with one another, having some deep conversations about our hopes and dreams and our aspirations for the future. My confidence in her grew and grew. I'd shared openly with her about my life. There was one bit of information I knew she needed to know about me if the relationship was to go to the next level, the lifetime plunge of marriage.

Cut back to the two of us sitting in my car in the parking lot at Samford. This was the big moment! I let her know I had something really important to tell her. She picked up quickly that it must have been "huge" because of the look on my face and the sound of my voice. I can just imagine what might have been running through her mind. Was I having a relationship with yet another girl behind her back? Had I killed someone, trying to keep it a big secret? I know she probably wasn't thinking about this last possibility, but it adds drama to the story.

The Breakdown

I began to speak, and I lost it! I was bawling my eyes out as I started to share something with her I had never told anyone before. No, it wasn't a criminal act or another girl-friend situation. I told her I was an emotional freak! I really felt like that. I began to describe some of the behaviors I'd struggled with since my childhood, behaviors that ruled my life. I was a "repeater." What's that, you ask? The clinical name for it is Obsessive Compulsive Disorder. Those who suffer from this do things over and over and over again— whether it's brushing hair or teeth, closing window curtains, or reading lines of a passage in a book. These are just a few examples. Those with the disorder are unable to stop the behavior for fear that something bad might happen. Believe it or not, at times the behavior gives them a sense of control. Does this sound crazy or what? I'd tried so hard to hide this over the years and I couldn't keep it hidden any longer. It was time for full disclosure. It was time to give her the full view. I had worked hard to show her the good side of me, but it was time to reveal "the other side."

What happened next really surprised me. It wasn't that she accepted what I had shared and wanted to help me deal with it—this was the response I had hoped for and believed would happen. The surprise was the relief I felt after telling her. It was as if this monster that had attached itself to me and haunted me over the years had finally let go. A weight had been removed. The confession had released me from a burden that had been holding me back. It was the beginning of my emotional healing.

Honesty

I opened up to Jennifer because I trusted her. You may be taken aback because of my openness with you. After all, I'm a pastor, and I'm telling you some intimate details of my life. More will come as you read. I've learned that there's power in honesty. It begins with taking a close look at ourselves, seeing who we really are. This is followed by allowing others to see inside us as we share the truth about who we really are. We disclose information. The word *disclose* means "to give information." For our purposes, it will mean voluntarily giving information about ourselves for the purpose of personal improvement. We become transparent when we disclose, allowing others to see inside. We really do give them a full view. We reveal those things that we've been trying to hide. Why would we do this? We'll do it when we believe the reward is worth the risk. We take the risk of sharing, knowing the possible benefit is great. The benefit is great! The benefit is a life of freedom. Secrets bind us, but the truth really does set us free.

God didn't create us to live loner lives, trying to handle our problems by ourselves. He created us to be in community, helping each other grow and achieve victory over struggles. I believe that's exactly what God can help you do through reading this book. Although I might not know you personally, I want to act as if I'm your friend. I want to reveal some issues in my life in the hopes that it will encourage you to share your problems with others. Yes, it might be embarrassing. It won't be easy. In fact, expect it to be difficult. Who said life was piece of cake? Life isn't easy, but living it is worthwhile. God has a great plan for your life. He wants you to have great value. You'll feel valued when you know God can turn your weaknesses into strengths, using them to bring positive change to our world.

A Message That Went Right

This was the first of many moments when I faced my emotional "stuff" and shared it with others. I would eventually open up with other family members and counselors, but none of these experiences would prepare me for what would happen when I went public, sharing with the masses.

Our church began a ministry called Celebrate Recovery a few months ago. It was developed by Saddleback Church in California. The purpose of the group is to help people deal with their hurts, habits, and hang-ups. The leadership team in charge of the ministry asked me if I would deliver some messages during our weekend services to promote the ministry and encourage those who were in need to participate. I agreed and began preparing a series of sermons on emotions, a topic I had become very familiar with because of my past experiences.

I hadn't planned to be so open with the people of our church, but during the first message of the series I began to tell my story. It was a God thing! I couldn't believe what I was saying. After all, this was information which could have caused the people in the church to lose their willingness to follow my leadership. It can be tough to follow people who are emotional wrecks. Right? What would people think about their "screwed up" pastor? I was amazed at the response.

I didn't have an altar call, asking all of the messed up people to "out themselves" in front of the crowd. Instead, I prayed a prayer of encouragement. The service ended, and then it happened. Person after person began coming up to me and telling me about their own emotional lives, the struggles their spouses were having, and the struggles of their children. My sharing had encouraged people to begin the process of healing, seeking the help they needed. An unplanned transparent moment from a pastor had led to others becoming transparent themselves, finding release from secrets that were keeping them from living up to their God-given potential.

This event was the catalyst for the book you are now reading. God began to burden me about sharing my story with others to encourage them to become transparent themselves, finding relief and beginning the journey toward emotional health. It's my hope the information you read in this book will help you face your struggles and find the freedom that comes from openness. Transparency makes a difference. Full disclosure is worthwhile. Giving people a view of who you are exposes the issues that need attention. Let's get real about ourselves and open up. Let's admit who we are and do what we need to do to understand our problems. Let's learn what God has to say about us and discover what we are to do to be overcomers! Are you ready?

Chapter Two

In the Beginning

Then you will know the truth, and the truth will set you free.

John 8:32

The longer I live, the more convinced I am that all of us are "off" in one way or another. I know this is true of me. Evidently I'm not the only one who's had a difficult time with emotional issues. The statistics prove it. According to the National Institute of Mental Health,

- 19 million Americans suffer from anxiety disorders.
- 2.4 million adult Americans suffer from panic disorder.
- 3.3 million adult Americans suffer from Obsessive Compulsive Disorder.
- 5.2 million adult Americans suffer from Post Traumatic Stress Disorder.
- 5.3 million adult Americans suffer from Social phobias.
- 4 million adult Americans suffer from Generalized Anxiety Disorder.[1]

Where did our emotional challenges come from? We have our ancestors to thank for it. Adam and Eve set us on a course of struggle and heartache by inviting sin into our world. Mankind has been riding an emotional rollercoaster since that moment. We see the first evidence of mankind's emotional struggle immediately after the first act of disobedience before God. The Bible says,

> But the LORD God called to the man, "Where are you?" He answered, "I heard you in the garden, and I was afraid because I was naked; so I hid." And he said, "Who told you that you were naked? Have you eaten from the tree that I commanded you not to eat from?" The man said, "The woman you put here with me—she gave me some fruit from the tree, and I ate it." Then the LORD God said to the woman, "What is this you have done?" The woman said, "The serpent deceived me, and I ate.
>
> Genesis 3:9-13

The sin of Adam led to an emotional response. He was afraid. It was the first negative emotion. His emotional reaction was the evidence that something was "off." What's next? Let the blame game begin! When Adam and Eve were confronted with their mistake, the finger pointing started. Someone must be to blame for our wrong choices and incorrect emotions, right? Our tendency is to look to others and believe they're the cause of our problems instead of taking an honest look at ourselves to discover our own failures. The truth is, no one makes wrong choices for us and no one controls our emotions. It's all on us. In a way, this is liberating. Now that we know we're to blame, we know who needs our attention. We can stop spending all of our time trying to "fix" other people and start getting real about who we are and learning how to experience personal healing. If we don't, someone's going to get hurt.

Hurt

The indicator that emotions are unhealthy is "hurt." Healthy emotions encourage and restore while unhealthy emotions discourage and destroy. Our unhealthy emotions typically begin when we hurt ourselves first. We begin looking down on ourselves and devalue what God has created. These thoughts lead to self-destructive behaviors. If we don't deal with these feelings about ourselves, our emotions can lead us to harm others.

Let's get back to the story about the first family. Emotional problems ran in their household and we see how emotional issues began to have an effect on family members. Adam and Eve had two sons named Cain and Abel. We read their story in the fourth chapter of Genesis:

> Adam lay with his wife Eve, and she became pregnant and gave birth to Cain. She said, "With the help of the LORD I have brought forth a man." Later she gave birth to his brother Abel. Now Abel kept flocks, and Cain worked the soil. In the course of time Cain brought some of the fruits of the soil as an offering to the LORD. But Abel brought fat portions from some of the firstborn of his flock. The LORD looked with favor on Abel and his offering, but on Cain and his offering he did not look with favor. So Cain was very angry, and his face was downcast. Then the LORD said to Cain, "Why are you angry? Why is your face downcast? ⁷If you do what is right, will you not be accepted? But if you do not do what is right, sin is crouching at your door; it desires to have you, but you must master it." Now Cain said to his brother Abel,

21

"Let's go out to the field." And while they were in the field, Cain attacked his brother Abel and killed him. Then the LORD said to Cain, "Where is your brother Abel?" "I don't know," he replied. "Am I my brother's keeper?" The LORD said, "What have you done? Listen! Your brother's blood cries out to me from the ground. Now you are under a curse and driven from the ground, which opened its mouth to receive your brother's blood from your hand. When you work the ground, it will no longer yield its crops for you. You will be a restless wanderer on the earth."

Genesis 4:1-12

The Scripture teaches us that Cain was angry and downcast (another word for depressed). These were unhealthy emotions. We know this to be true because these emotions led him to hurt someone else—his brother. He had a "crouching sin" problem. God told Cain that sin was crouching at his door.

Sin crouches near unhealthy emotions. Our emotions cause us to begin thinking about ways to harm others. Somehow, we believe this will make us feel better. Consider Cain's behavior. It appears he was setting up the scene to kill his brother by inviting him out to the field. Like Cain, if we don't stop these feelings, we'll begin fantasizing about ways to hurt others and will live out these fantasies, inflicting pain. This is sin. Obedient behavior is loving behavior. It protects others and builds them up. Disobedient behavior is self-centered behavior. It destroys others and tears them down.

Confession

What do we do if we find ourselves experiencing unhealthy emotions? Great question! Let's think about Adam and Eve once again. Although they blamed others for their mistakes, they did something very important. They were transparent and honest about their disobedience. This is known as confession. Their confession caused the relationship between them and God to be restored. Cain, however, refused to be honest with Him. God confronted Cain with his sin by asking him about the location of his brother. Cain responded by saying, "I don't know. Am I my brother's keeper?" God gave him an opportunity to "fess up," but he refused. The result was a life of wandering. It happened because he refused to take an honest look at his own life and admit his mistakes. We wander aimlessly when we don't confess and face our problems and spend our time trying to make sense of a life built on difficulties we refuse to acknowledge.

The first step toward experiencing emotional health is confession—giving a true and honest description of our struggles. Through confession, our relationship with God is restored. Through confession, our relationships with others can be restored. Through confession, our emotional lives begin the journey of being restored. Jesus made an awesome statement when He said, "The truth will set you free" (John 8:32). We begin the process of being set free when we're tired of a life of destructive thoughts and actions and long for a life of peace and joy.

The Causes

Where do these emotional behaviors come from? There are three primary causes. The first is physical. Physician Clark Gerhart dealt with emotions in his book, *Say Goodbye to Stubborn Sin*. He writes, "While we like to think of emotions as being 'the way we feel,' they really are the result of a series of complex neurological signals that combine to give us that feeling."[2] He goes on to write, "The emotions are not ends, in and of themselves—they're part of how your brain decides upon a proper response."[3] Some experience a chemical imbalance in the brain. This imbalance trig-

23

gers an emotional behavior which is often unwanted. Those who suffer from this physical problem find great relief from medical professionals who help them find balance once again through medication. By the way, I'm included in this group.

The second is cognitive. It's how we think. Our beliefs about certain events—past, present, or future—affect our emotions. Those who experience emotional problems because of this find relief in changing the way they think. Some even seek professional help. The expert assists them through cognitive therapy. In this process, attention is given to our thoughts and beliefs.

The third is spiritual. Although this cause is third in our list, it really is first in importance. Our spiritual lives are centered around faith, which is a heart issue. Faith is developed from our beliefs about God, ourselves, and our world. If our faith is off, we begin to place our trust in things that let us down, including ourselves. If we're let down, we easily become emotionally imbalanced and begin to act out in emotionally and spiritually unhealthy ways. Adam and Cain are great examples of people who experienced emotional problems because of spiritual issues of faith.

There's a strong connection between the cognitive—what we think—and our spiritual life—what we trust in. A person who struggles emotionally should consider all three elements—physical, cognitive, and spiritual—when trying to understand their emotional situation. I've considered all three factors in addressing my emotional challenges. It's been a tough process. I'm a person who has a tremendous amount of willpower, and I tend to accomplish what I am determined to do. I approached my emotional problems with the same attitude. This began with the mental part of emotional health. To better understand who I was, I formally studied psychology, receiving a bachelor's degree. Through my studies I learned some mental exercises which were helpful in controlling my behaviors. Unfortunately, they didn't give me complete relief. I needed more. The next step was to participate in formal counseling to help me form realistic expectations and to better understand who I was. Sounds good so far, right? Well, learning more in these areas didn't heal my emotional problems. This led me to deal with spiritual issues. I needed to make sure my trust was in God. Instead of putting my trust in God, I had been trusting in my willpower alone to overcome these problems. My faith was in the wrong place. Although I had begun taking an honest look at myself, I continued to experience negative emotions. This finally caused me to consider the third emotional factor—my physical condition.

Not too long ago, I found myself in a deep depression I couldn't "will" away. I'd been struggling for years with severe mood swings, either being really up and living like "Mr. Enthusiasm," or being really down and depressed. I talked with my wife, and off to the family doctor we went. It was really more of a struggle than this, but I'll get into the details a little later. I had hoped I could handle my "emotional funk" on my own, but I finally realized I couldn't and that I needed to seek medical help. I told the doctor about my up and down tendencies, wanting him to give me a magic pill. No such luck! Instead of giving me medicine, he referred me to a psychiatrist. He reasoned that if he gave me medication, he might give me the wrong prescription and make matters worse. He told me I needed to see a specialist. I'll be honest, when I heard the word *psychiatrist*, my body tensed up. He gave me the doctor's name and I left the office. As I was walking out the doctor's office, I threw away the referral. I had already determined not to make the appointment. I, like many, didn't want to have the stigma of being a "mental patient." I was disappointed and my hopes were dashed.

Buyer

Not only did I make a bad decision in not going to see "the specialist," but I also made another poor choice. Before I tell you more about my bad choice, I need to fill you in on a pattern in my life. I get fixated on stuff, normally material stuff. It's like my mind has to find something to obsess about. I've been this way for as long as I can remember. It's a real problem because I don't think rationally in these moments and I purchase things on impulse. Sometimes I can afford them, and other times not.

We lived in Jacksonville several years ago. My wife taught school and I was a student minister. I had a day off during the week to compensate for the many hours I worked at night and on the weekends, but my wife didn't have this privilege. She worked every weekday. It was a really dangerous thing for me to have an off day by myself. It wasn't only an "off day," it was a "what can I buy today?" day. On one of those days I went to the store and saw a really cool patio set out of my price range. We had purchased a home that had a huge porch, but no furniture. I thought to myself, *You know, that furniture would look really awesome on our patio.* The salesperson informed me I could get ten percent off if I applied for a Pier One credit card. Guess what I did? I applied for a Pier One credit card. By the end of the day, the furniture was on the porch. Imagine the surprise when Jennifer came home. If that wasn't bad enough, my mother-in-law was also living with us at the time. I faced two women who couldn't believe what I'd done.

Typically, I'm pretty good about money and don't get the family into too much financial trouble. Actually, my "risk-taking" has paid off for us in some situations. Unfortunately, this has not always been true. Let the buying continue! I love boats. You've probably heard the statement before that the two happiest days in a boater's life are the days he buys it and the day he sells it. I know firsthand that this is absolutely a true statement. At least it is for me. You'd think I'd learned my lesson after the number of boats I went through. There have been six all together. It doesn't sound as bad when you spread them over the twenty years Jennifer and I have been married. The purchase of the last one was an emotional wake-up call. This is the bad choice I referred to earlier.

To find some relief from the latest funk, I began to fixate on buying a new boat. It didn't take too long after the purchase to know I had made a big mistake. I had justified why I needed it. All of us need an escape, right? I know others have stressful jobs, but the ministry can be stress overload. You're on call twenty-four hours a day and there are very few times where you are free from being around people. Don't get me wrong, I enjoy being with people, but after a while you need a break. This was going to be my break. It was going to be the "thing" that would help me get out of my emotional funk, allowing me some alone time and family time. I had justified why I needed it and then came the justification for how I could afford it. Where there's a will there's a way! Somehow in my deciphering, I thought I had determined a way it could be mine. The only thing left was to make the sales pitch to Jennifer to convince her why we needed to make the purchase. She gave in and the boat was mine. There was only one problem! What I thought we could afford, we couldn't, and buyer's remorse set in.

Three months passed, and I found myself more discouraged than I'd ever been before. Jennifer desperately wanted to help me. She ran across a book by Dr. Paul Meir called *Blue Genes*. It included information about the many emotional diseases that people suffered from. In it, he provided a detailed description of the disorders and behaviors of those who suffered from them. Jennifer began reading and came across a section on bipolar disorder. She, like me, didn't realize there were different types of bipolar disorder.

I knew I had severe up and down tendencies, but I didn't consider them to be extreme. After all, I didn't get so low that I wanted to end my life, a symptom of those who suffer from Type One Bipolar Disorder. She came to find out that there is also a Type Two. As she read, she realized she was reading about me. It was like someone had interviewed me and written a description of my behavior in the book. She showed me what was written, and I was blown away.

My wife called our family physician, got the name of the psychiatrist, made the appointment, and told me I was going. Kind of bossy, huh? I reluctantly obeyed because I was afraid of what I would be getting into. I know that's not something you typically hear a pastor say. After all, with God we should have no fear, right? This tells you where my faith was on that day—obviously in the wrong place. I will say it was one of the best decisions of my life. The psychiatrist tested me and confirmed what I had expected. It was Bipolar Type Two. He taught me about the genealogical influence of the disease and said it was a physical problem that occurred because of the imbalance of chemicals in the brain. I also learned from him that my risk-taking and my buying behavior were classic symptoms of the disease. I was amazed to learn that many CEOs and key leaders of major organizations suffer from the same disease. Their risk-taking has paid off for them. But they, like me, need help to ensure we don't go over the edge. I wasn't healed, but I was relieved. My behavior had a name, and now I could do something about it. Just knowing what I had began to change my mood.

There's more to the story. I have four children—three girls and a boy. One of my girls is a carbon copy of me. Not physically. That would be a really cruel thing for God to do to her. She's a carbon copy emotionally. Both my wife and I began to notice the same symptoms in her. She was expressing these emotions not only around family, but also around friends. Her moods were severe, so much so that her friends started calling her "Moo" (short for "moody"). Believe it or not, she embraced the name and thought it was cool. I kept the appointment, not only because I wanted to find relief, but also because I wanted to set a good example for her and help her in any way I could.

I need to address another issue before I move on. Some believe we can be healed if we have enough faith that God will heal us. I believe in the miraculous work of God. I've seen God heal people because of their faith in Him. Some say we aren't healed because we don't have enough faith. There are times when this may be true. However, there are also times when this isn't true. Although God chooses to heal some who have faith and believe in His healing power, He doesn't heal everyone who has faith. This reminds me of the apostle Paul, a faithful example, who struggled with a thorn in the flesh. Many believe this thorn was a physical problem. Check out what he wrote about his condition:

> To keep me from becoming conceited because of these surpassingly great revelations, there was given me a thorn in my flesh, a messenger of Satan, to torment me. [8]Three times I pleaded with the Lord to take it away from me. [9]But he said to me, "My grace is sufficient for you, for my power is made perfect in weakness." Therefore I will boast all the more gladly about my weaknesses, so that Christ's power may rest on me. [10]That is why, for Christ's sake, I delight in weaknesses, in insults, in hardships, in persecutions, in difficulties. For when I am weak, then I am strong.
>
> 2 Corinthians 12:7-10

Paul called his "thorn" a "messenger of Satan." That is exactly what physical illness is. It is something that has occurred because of the influence of Satan on humanity.

As we have already learned, sin brought physical disease into the world, which causes destruction. If faith was all that was required, we could master every disease and live forever physically. This is simply not the case. God told us we wouldn't live forever physically. He numbered our days. Although Paul asked God to take his thorn away, God didn't do it. He didn't heal Paul for a reason. It caused Paul to rely more heavily on God. It was a faith-building experience. I've learned there are times that God will also do the same for us. Believe it or not, this is a blessing and not a curse.

Relief

Back to my story! I'm finding relief through medication and nutritional supplements that have been helpful in putting my brain back in balance. This hasn't been the only solution for me as I've moved toward good emotional health. I must continue to have my faith and my mind in order. My condition, like Paul's, has become a faith-builder for me.

Some need medical, cognitive, and spiritual help in dealing with emotions while others need only to learn how to change their thought patterns and focus their trust on God. The most important of these is keeping our focus on the spiritual by learning how we can trust in God. The solution to correcting how we think is spiritual in nature. In her book, *Breaking the Grip of Dangerous Emotions,* Janet Maccaro writes that "research has uncovered one of the greatest healing miracles of all time—spirituality." Our spiritual lives not only affect us emotionally, but spiritually as well. She went on to write that "more than three hundred studies confirm that people of faith are healthier than nonbelievers and less likely to die prematurely from any cause." She taught that "having faith can also speed recovery from physical and mental illness, surgery and addiction."[4] Finally, she shared that "faith...gives you a sense of peace and an ability to help you look beyond your present problems with hope, which can reduce stress and lower your risk of anxiety and depression."[5] Here's a Tim paraphrase: Faith heals!

If you are a person of faith in Christ, this should give you hope. You may be anxious and stressed out, but you have within you what you need to overcome this problem by refocusing on the solution for your problems—God. The key to properly expressing ourselves emotionally comes from having the mind of Christ, a mind that is fully devoted to God. Paul knew this. He gave the instruction that "the spiritual man makes judgments about all things, but he himself is not subject to any man's judgment: "For who has known the mind of the Lord that he may instruct him?" But we have the mind of Christ" (1 Corinthians 2:15-16). Who is this mind of Christ?

The Self-Coach

We need help changing our emotions, and God has given us just who we need. God has given us the mind of Christ— His Spirit. He works in a powerful way, confirming our correct thoughts and convicting us of those that are incorrect. God confirms what we think when we trust in Him and convicts us of our thoughts when we don't trust in Him. The Holy Spirit is given to us as a life coach.

Adele B. Lynn, an expert in the area of emotional intelligence, suggested that we benefit from having a "self-coach" in her book, *The EQ Difference: A Powerful Plan for Putting Emotional Intelligence to Work*. She writes,

I am proposing the notion of a self-coach. To help improve our emotional intelligence. By creating a self-coach, we would have someone to consult, someone to whisper in our ear, and someone to advise us about the sometimes treacherous path of human interaction. The self-coach I'm proposing lives within each of us, because I believe that we each have a higher capacity that we could tap into to examine our behaviors and determine if we are acting in line with our intentions.[6]

Lynn approaches the "self-coach" from a secular perspective. There's a great difference between a secular point of view and a godly viewpoint concerning the self-coach we need. God provides His Spirit to us to help us become self-aware and have a clear understanding of who we are and what we need to become. He's given us a self-coach not to achieve "our" intentions, but to achieve "His" intentions. Lynn taught that "the self-coach isn't there to impose guilt when you've done something wrong, but rather to help you learn from your experiences."[7] The coach can help us see our mistakes. We don't need a coach who causes us to feel guilty; we need a coach who leads us to feel sorry. Our sorrow over what we've done or become brings change. God's coach helps us see the failures we've made and moves us toward correction that changes what we experience. Paul taught what it is. He writes, "The mind of sinful man is death, but the mind controlled by the Spirit is life and peace..." (Romans 8:6).

God wants you to overcome negative emotions to become a reflection of who He is. He is the God of peace and joy. A life of peace brings joy. I want to experience joy—what about you? I invite you to take a journey with me as we learn how to experience the peace that gives us joy in life. Ask God right now to begin the healing process in your mind by teaching you how to fully trust in Him:

God,
Teach me what I need to know to experience emotional healing so I can lead others to trust in you.

Chapter Three

Get Smart

Instruct a wise man and he will be wiser still; teach a
righteous man and he will add to his learning.

Proverbs 9:9

If you had a choice between being emotionally smart or
emotionally ignorant, which would you choose? No-
brainer, right? The truth is we all make this decision. We
are to be smart emotionally. This happens when we become
aware of our emotions and how they influence us. When
I think about the word *intelligent*, my mind flashes back
to college. Maybe you can relate. You've taken a test, the
professor or teacher gives it back to you, and you see the
grade. It's not exactly what you hoped for. In fact, it doesn't
even come close. To make yourself feel better, you reason to
yourself, "This grade doesn't reflect my real intelligence."
Yeah, right! Well, maybe this is true.

Researchers have discovered there are factors that determine our success in a society other than our academic knowledge. Does this give you hope or what? Studies show there
are other abilities that make a greater difference. They have
to do with our emotions. What do we need to know?

Our Emotions Guide Us

The very root of the word *emotions* is a Latin verb which means "to move."[8] Our actions direct our lives. They also prepare us to respond in certain ways to deal with specific situations. Let me give you an example. When we become angry, our bodies physically change to prepare us to protect ourselves. This physical reaction occurs because of our emotional condition. What we do with this emotional response makes the difference in our behavior. We become emotional and then we act, and the result can either be positive or negative depending on our behavior.

Although there are many emotions, three are basic. David Stoop, who holds a Ph.D. and is an expert in the field, dealt with these in his book, *You Are What You Think*. Here's the list:

- **Love** - the emotion that moves us toward someone or something.[9] We're drawn to those who show love to us. We long to be with those who prove they care for us. There's a positive feeling experienced when love is present.
- **Anger** - the emotion that moves us toward someone or something, but it moves us against the object.[10] We're drawn to them, not because of a positive feeling, but because of a negative feeling.
- **Fear** - the emotion that moves us away from someone or something.[11] We back away for self-protection.

The Scriptures teach us about all three. God showed the emotions of anger and love. The Psalmist writes, "The LORD is gracious and compassionate, slow to anger and rich in love" (Psalm 145:8). What a great promise! This doesn't mean He doesn't show His anger. Over and over again, especially in the Old Testament, we see God act out in anger.

However, it is anger expressed for a positive purpose. We also know He is loving. The greatest example of God's love is the gift He provides us in His Son, Jesus Christ. Jesus says, "For God so loved the world that he gave his one and only Son, that whoever believes in him shall not perish but have eternal life" (John 3:16).

Fear is also found in the Bible. Peter writes, "Who is going to harm you if you are eager to do good? But even if you should suffer for what is right, you are blessed. "Do not fear what they fear; do not be frightened" (1 Peter 3:13-14). God speaks of fear when he says, "Do not fear me..." (Malachi 3:5b). Fear paralyzes us and is the basis for many emotional problems. Fear is the beginning of anxiety, and anxiety can become emotionally crippling. Not a good place to be! We need to choose our emotions wisely. The best choice is love over fear. John taught that "There is no fear in love. But perfect love drives out fear..." (1 John 4:18).

Stoop pointed out that every feeling we have in life is either a pure example of one of the emotions or a blending of them. He taught that we can think of the emotions like the primary colors of red, blue, and yellow. All other colors are a blending of these primary colors. In the same way, all emotions are a blending of love, fear, and anger.[12] These three emotions are the source of other feelings. For example, my love may cause me to feel happy or peaceful. My anger may cause me to feel rejected or stupid. My fear may cause me to feel anxious and stressed.

The Two Minds

Remember the words of the apostle Paul. He writes, "The mind of sinful man is death, but the mind controlled by the Spirit is life and peace; the sinful mind is hostile to God. It does not submit to God's law, nor can it do so. Those controlled by the sinful nature cannot please God" (Romans

8:6-8). The Scripture teaches us something critical about life. We need to be concerned about who controls our minds. There are two minds at work in us:

- **The Rational Mind**. Our rational mind is the mind that thinks. The Scripture we just read relates to our rational mind. This mind is used to understand the events that are happening around us. It's important to think proper thoughts about the circumstances of life because our rational minds guide us in life. The rational mind is the catalyst for emotional behavior. Our emotions follow our thoughts. The Bible teaches us that "for as he thinketh in his heart, so is he..." (Proverbs 23:7, KJV). The rational mind also triggers the other mind.
- **The Emotional Mind**. The emotional mind is the mind that feels. There are times when the rational mind and the emotional mind work together and support one another, but there are also times when they deliver different messages. As a pastor, I've dealt with many people who've experienced tragedy. Time passes and I have the opportunity to talk with them about how they've been coping. Some tell me they're struggling. Others have said they're doing well. This appears to be true because their emotions back up their statement. Others say they're fine but begin to show their sorrow emotionally. They say one thing from their rational mind, thinking they should be strong, but their emotional mind has a much different reaction.

If we're not careful, we can allow our emotional mind to take over our rational mind. When we do this, we begin acting out without rationally thinking about our behavior. We feel first, and then we respond without deliberately thinking. Imagine this situation. A mother who's been struggling with a disrespectful child comes in from work. She's having a calm conversation when the child begins to speak in an abusive way toward another family member. The mother, who's not a violent person, slaps the child without thinking. When she looks back on the event, she can't believe what she did. She feels like she was out of control. What happened? The wrong mind was in control.

Have you ever "lost it" in anger and acted out against someone, not using your rational mind to think about what you were doing? How do we overcome this? The solution is to prepare for these highly sensitive emotional events. What we do with our rational minds in non-stressful times helps us make better decisions in stressful times. For example, if we continue to train our rational mind to flee when the stress level rises, we take ourselves out of the volatile situation. This allows things to calm down so that cooler heads can make good decisions to resolve the problem. If we don't train our rational mind to make wise decisions in times of conflict, we fight. If we fight, things get messy. Are things messy for you?

Emotions and Circumstances

Think about the story you just read about the mother and the child. Did the child's behavior make the mother respond in a violent way? Was it the child's fault? Our emotions and behaviors don't depend on our circumstances. It's tempting to believe our emotions are dependent upon what happens to us. Those who believe this spend their time attempting to control circumstances to bring about the desired emotional outcome.

What does this mean to us? It means you don't make me angry; I make me angry. Being angry is not the only emotion available to me. If you don't make me angry and I do make me angry, then what is it about me that makes me angry? What controls my emotions?

The Power of Our Belief System

Stoop illustrates what happens to us emotionally by using three letters—A, B, and C. Let's take a look at what A, B, and C represent:

- **A – The Activating Event.** This represents the situation. Someone says or does something to us.
- **B – Beliefs.** What we think about the situation.
- **C – The Consequence.**[13] How we respond through emotions and behaviors.

Many people blame their emotional response on the activating event. In other words, A=C. Take a look at the following example:

- A – (Activating event) A snake comes across a room toward me.
- C – (The emotional consequence that comes out of me) I am afraid (the primary emotion).

I may think the snake coming across the room toward me is the reason I'm afraid. This isn't correct. Why? There's a "B." What we believe about the event becomes real to us and our emotions respond accordingly. The correct formula is: A + B = C.

Let's add the B into this illustration:

- A – (Activating event) A snake comes across a room toward me.
- B – (Belief) I believe the snake is going to bite me and harm me.
- C – (The emotional consequence that comes out of me) I'm afraid (the primary emotion).

What happens when our belief changes? The consequence (behavior) also changes. Let's think back on the snake situation. This is a good example because I can't stand snakes. If a snake came across the room toward me, I would see it and believe it was going to bite me and, out of the emotion of fear, scream like a twelve-year-old girl and run out of the room because of my anxiety. How could things change? Let's imagine this really happened and, after being frightened, I decide to go to a class on snake handling. I learn that snakes aren't that bad after all. Upon completion of the class, the same snake comes across the same room and now I see it and believe it would make a great pet. I move toward it and pick it up. It's the same snake. I'm the same person. But I now have a different belief system. This is illustrated below:

- A – (Activating event) A snake comes across a room toward me.
- B – (Belief) I believe the snake is friendly and would make a great pet.
- C – (The emotional consequence that comes out of me) I'm happy because I believe the snake will add value to my life.

Imagine a third situation with the snake. How would it change my behavior if there was a previous event that occurred with a snake? Imagine that on a past camping trip a poisonous snake came into the camp and bit one of my children, which had led to their death. Also imagine that I remain emotionally upset over this event and am angry at the snake's action. With this past history, I'm now in a room and a snake comes into the room (the activating event). I believe all snakes are evil because of what the snake did to my child (my belief). Therefore, I move toward the snake and cut off its head (the consequence). This situation is illustrated below:

- A – (Activating event) A snake comes across a room toward me.
- B – (Belief) I believe all snakes are evil.
- C – (The emotional consequence that comes out of me) I move toward the snake aggressively and cut off its head.

Remember the three emotions. In fear, I move away (the first snake situation). In love, I move toward it to make a positive connection (the second snake situation). In anger, I move toward it, but I move against it to inflict pain (the third snake situation). We respond to all events with these emotions depending upon our beliefs. We can be afraid of the event, we can look to the event as something positive that will improve our lives, or we can be angry at the event. Our beliefs bring about the outcome. You respond to situations that are happening around you. To change your emotions, change your beliefs.

Our responses are based on how we choose to interpret events. Remember, the Bible says, "For as he thinketh in his heart, so is he..." (Proverbs 23:7, KJV). Jeremiah is a good example for us. He experienced depression because of a belief. We learn about his feelings toward God. He writes, "He has walled me in so I cannot escape; he has weighed me down with chains. Even when I call out or cry for help, he shuts out my prayer. He has barred my way with blocks of stone; he has made my paths crooked" (Jeremiah 3:7-9). He was depressed because of what he believed about God and what God was doing. His feelings changed when he changed his belief. He later states, "I well remember them, and my soul is downcast within me. Yet this I call to mind and therefore I have hope: Because of the LORD'S great love we are not consumed, for his compassions never fail. They are new every morning; great is your faithfulness. I say to myself, 'The LORD is my portion; therefore I will wait for him'" (Jeremiah 3:23-24). He called something new to his mind. He said something new to himself. It's time for you to say something new to yourself.

Another great example for us is the event in the Old Testament involving the spies who were sent into the Promised Land. God had secured the release of the people of Israel from Egypt. Moses led them to the border of the Promised Land, and twelve spies were sent into the land to check it out. Ten went into the land and became afraid of what they saw. They came back and said the people were of great size and could not be overcome. That's what they believed. This belief caused them to make the suggestion that the people of Israel play it safe and not go into the land. Two went into the land and became confident about what they saw. They came back and shared with the people that God would give them victory. They believed in God and trusted in Him. They were excited about taking the risk. Ten were afraid and led the people away. They were trusting in their abilities alone, and the consequence was forty years of wandering in the wilderness. Two wanted to go forward and were excited about what God could do because of their trust in Him. They went into the same land. They were from the same nation. Both groups of people experienced the same thing but had different beliefs, which led to different emotional responses.

We are transformed by a change of mind. Paul writes, "Do not conform any longer to the pattern of this world, but be transformed by the renewing of your mind. Then you will be able to test and approve what God's will is—his good, pleasing and perfect will" (Romans 12:2). To renew our minds, we must put new thoughts into our minds. In other words, we must change the message we're telling ourselves. The old message has led to our failure and to our broken condition. The new message can bring healing and restoration. Don't you want to know how? Read on! I hope the information in the next chapter rocks your world like it has mine. It's time to be restored.

God,
I confess to You that I having been having wrong beliefs about life. I need Your help to transform my mind. I ask You now to help keep my mind on what is true, noble, right, pure, lovely, admirable, excellent, and praiseworthy. I thank You that You confirm my heart when my mind is right and You convict my heart when my mind is wrong. Please help me to experience life and peace. In Jesus' name, Amen.

Chapter Four

Restored

Accept instruction from his mouth and lay up his
words in your heart. If you return to the Almighty,
you will be restored...

Job 22:22-23

I'm a hurricane survivor! Living in the state of Florida on
the coast for most of my life has put me in or near the
path of several storms. The terrible year of 2004, which saw
several hurricanes come through the state, caused many resi-
dents to become really antsy or nervous about what might
come. Although our area was not hit directly, we felt the
winds as the edge of two storms barely missed us.

When a storm comes, emergency management officials
make a really big deal about being prepared—and with
good reason. One of the items every emergency kit should
contain is a flashlight. It's pretty obvious why. If the power
fails, there's a really good chance you'll need light through
another device to stay safe as you make your way around the
house. It's really not a very cool thing to be in the dark with
winds howling in the middle of the night and not being able
to see how to make it to the bathroom. Bummer! It's also
really not cool to have a flashlight and try to turn it on during

the storm only to discover that it's broken. Wisdom says test it before you need it.

God created us for a purpose. Our purpose is to make a positive eternal difference. We do this when we reveal God in a dark world, leading people toward Him. We become a light for Him. Jesus illustrated this to us by talking about a lamp in a dark house. He says,

> You are the light of the world. A city on a hill cannot be hidden. Neither do people light a lamp and put it under a bowl. Instead they put it on its stand, and it gives light to everyone in the house. In the same way, let your light shine before men, that they may see your good deeds and praise your Father in heaven.
>
> Matthew 5:14-16

When we show God's light, we praise our Father in heaven. Why? Because we have become like Him. How do we show this light? Great question! Jesus told us how when He spoke. We show God's light by performing good deeds. So what are good deeds? Serving those around us. If we show our love through service, we produce what we were intended to produce. If we don't, we're broken and need to be restored. Because we're broken, our light is shut off. We've turned our love inward and don't aim it outward. Love aimed inward is darkness and love aimed outward is light. How does this relate to our emotions? This inward love (self-centeredness) is the root cause of many unhealthy emotions. People don't see God through destructive emotional behavior. They bring discouragement (darkness). They need restoration. Let's learn how.

I love watching those shows on the Speed Channel that take a clunker of a car and completely restore it into one that looks brand new. They show the condition of the car before the makeover—all broken down and a complete mess. Then the miracle happens. (Don't be judgmental. I know it's not a "real" miracle!). I sit in amazement staring at the finished product—a beautiful piece of art. If you saw the cars before the restoration, you would almost believe there was no hope. This really isn't true. They just needed the right person to come along to give it a new lease on life.

I share all of this because many feel as though there is no hope for their future. They believe they can't be restored. Not true! They, like the car, just need the right person to come along to help them with their emotional makeover. It's God! There's something cool about hope. What is it? Hope has to do with the future. If we see the future as bright, we have hope. However, if we see the future as bleak, we're discouraged. Both hope and discouragement have to do with what we see coming our way.

Here's something really important to grasp. You either live with hope or you live with discouragement. These are your two choices. If you live with hope, your emotions follow and you become healthy. These healthy emotions result in positive actions, which can lead to service—causing you to make a positive eternal difference. Your light is shining. If you live with discouragement, your emotions follow and you become unhealthy. These unhealthy emotions result in negative actions which come from being consumed with oneself. These behaviors cause you to make a negative eternal difference. You don't serve others, you lash out. We've reverted back to living like we don't know God. The key then is to do what is necessary to bring hope into your life and kill the discouragement you feel. I have good news. You're about to learn how to do just that. There are four elements that are involved in the restoration process. We must do the following:

Rewind

We must rewind. I call this the time machine effect. Wouldn't it be awesome if we could physically go back in time and change our decisions? If I had this opportunity, I know I would make some different choices (like the boat decision). I've made some choices in my past that have not only hurt me, but have also hurt others. My light didn't shine. Going back in time would be nice, but we can't. However, we can go back to those events—not physically—but in our minds. In fact, to change from discouragement to hope, we must go back to those events in our minds. There's a reason for this. We need to see our failures, learn from them, and prepare ourselves to face similar situations in the future so we can make the right choices. I want to help you go back in time.

Think about a situation when you failed. We can learn from this experience and prepare ourselves to make better choices in the future. To do this, we need to follow some specific steps:

- Step 1 – See what was occurring just prior to the failure. There were some circumstances that were happening that set you on a course which would ultimately lead to your failure. What were they? The circumstances led to something happening within you. What was it? To discover this, we must follow the next step.
- Step 2 – Remember what you were thinking about the circumstance that led to your failure. What did you believe? When faced with a situation, your mind begins to process what is happening around you and you begin to form an opinion. Your thinking may have only been about how you were being negatively affected by the situation. Your thoughts may

have only been about yourself. It's the self-centered thing again. Your self-centered thoughts led you in a bad direction, bringing about failure. If this is what occurred, we need to see it for what it is. We must own up to the fact that our thoughts were wrong, not right. If you don't see that your thoughts were wrong, you can't be corrected. This thinking leads us to experience something. To discover what it is, we must follow the next step.

- Step 3 – Feel the emotions you were feeling just prior to the failure. Remember, your emotions follow your thinking. Because this is true, your thoughts lead you to experience either healthy or unhealthy feelings. This is important to grasp because of what our emotions tell us about what we've been thinking. Get this—if we feel because we think, then we can see if we are thinking properly by noticing the way we feel. Cool! If our emotions are off, there's a reason for this. Again, many unhealthy feelings come from self-centered thinking. Healthy emotions come from our being concerned about the person who is coming against us. If there was failure, your emotions were unhealthy. You need to see this for what it is. You need to own up to this fact. If you don't, you can't correct your problem. It's time to take another step.

- Step 4 – See the failure. Let's follow the progression— we think, then we feel, then we act. The emotions you feel lead to the activities you perform. This can be negative or positive. Because there was failure, you experienced negative emotions that brought about selfish behavior which shut your light off. You've committed a crime. I know that sounds kind of heavy, but it's true. You've broken the commands of God. Jesus tells us the two commands we are to follow: "'...Love the Lord your God with all your heart and with all your soul and with all your mind.' This is the first and greatest commandment. And the second is like it: 'Love your neighbor as yourself'" (Matthew 22:37-39). Those who love God first also show love to their neighbor. This comes from a selfless heart. If you don't follow these commands, you become a spiritual criminal. This isn't a good place to be. You need to see it for what it is. You must own up to your failure. If you don't own up to your failure, there cannot be correction. This leads us to take another step.

- Step 5 – Feel the emotions you felt just after the failure. We think, then we feel, then we act, then we feel again. Your changing your future behavior is dependent upon the feeling you have about your failure. The feeling that brings about change is called remorse. There is another brokenness we must consider. We're to have a broken spirit. Read what the Psalmist writes about this: "The sacrifices of God are a broken spirit; a broken and contrite heart, O God, you will not despise" (Psalm 51:17). This attitude of the heart is a sacrifice before God. We give up our feelings aimed at the world and we now have feelings aimed at God. There is one more step to take.

How about a personal story? I confess I've been a criminal. I'm talking about being someone who has broken a law of our land. Before you get too judgmental on me, if you are a driver, there's a good chance you've done the same thing. You probably know what it is by now. I was a speeder. On one particular occasion, which means there must have been multiple incidents, Jennifer and I were traveling from college to her home on one of our school breaks. We were traveling down Highway 19, which goes through several small towns, one of which is called Cross City. I like to call it "Speed Trap

City." I slowed down as we went through town, but as the speed limit began to increase, so did I. My foot pushed on the pedal and I accelerated back to the speed I was traveling before—which was over the speed limit. I quickly came up on another car and passed it. I would later find out it was also speeding.

You may be wondering how I know that. After all, I didn't have a speed gun in my car to know how fast he was going. Let me explain. About the time I passed the car, I noticed some blue lights come up behind my car. You got it—the cops! In this case, the cop. He pulled me over and immediately told me to stay right where I was. Because I'm a really wise man, I stayed right where I was. He proceeded to chase down the car I had passed. I could see them up the highway. He obviously must have given him (or her—I know you women speed, too) a ticket because of the length of time he spent with the driver. Then he came back to my car.

Now to another part of the story! My major was psychology and I had just taken a class which included instruction on the power of our body language. One of the lessons was on how we express honesty by showing someone your palms. You put your hands up in the air with palms facing the person you're trying to convince. What a great time to test out this new information I had just learned at school. I could use my new emotional intelligence for a personal benefit. Here's how the conversation went:

He asked, "Son, why were you going so fast?"

My hands immediately went up into the air, palms facing him, and I said, "Sir, we just came through town and I noticed the speed limit signs were telling me it was okay to increases my speed, so I began to speed up. While I was speeding up, I was talking to my fiancée (trying to play the fiancé card) and I wasn't paying attention to how fast I was going. That's when I saw you come up behind us. I didn't realize I was going as fast as I was going."

He stood there for a minute and finally said, "Don't do it again," got in his car, and drove off. It worked! I had gotten out of the ticket.

You're probably already storing this information in your brain so you can use it the next time you're pulled over. If you're a cop, you'll never let anyone get away with this again. Here's the problem with this situation. I put my hands up in the air to communicate that I was honest, but I lied and I felt guilty. I purposefully had increased my speed to the same speed I had been driving, which was illegal.

What's the point? We should know we're guilty and feel sorry because we know we're wrong when we commit a crime as believers. It's an awesome experience. Here's why: We feel sorrow because God's Spirit is telling us what we did was wrong. My feeling sorrow can be evidence I know God. If I respond appropriately, my life begins to change because I now turn away from being a lawbreaker and toward God. I don't want to have this feeling again. There's a final step:

- Step 6 – Think about how you feel. We now process in our minds the decisions we should make. Because we don't like how we feel, we begin to think about what we can do to avoid it. We've come full circle. Look at the diagram. We think, feel, act, feel, and think again.

The Think Cycle

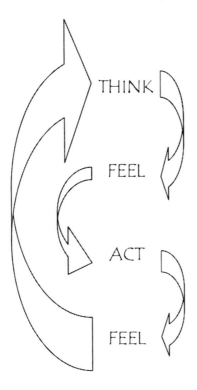

To change our behavior, we must change our thinking. God loves it when we feel remorse because it causes us to process in our minds why we feel the way we do and what we should have done in the situation.

This happens quite often in family situations. Maybe you can relate. There have been times in my life when I've allowed my thinking to steer me in the wrong direction, especially in my relationship with my kids. Kids will be kids, right? There are moments when I think kids should act like adults. How's that for an unrealistic expectation? They have a tendency to be selfish and not put much thought into how their behavior affects those around them. My children are no different. I can think of times, one in particular, when I heard them arguing and just being flat-out mean to one another. I began to think, *How can they be so stinkin' inconsiderate of other people in the family?* The longer I thought about it, the angrier I became. In anger, I reacted in a really ugly, ungodly way. Remorse immediately set in and I began to think about what I'd done and how I'd affected them. I began to think about their life in the future and wondered if this would be one of the thoughts that would keep coming to mind about their childhood. It really bothered me—big time! I determined in my mind never to act like that again when a similar situation arose. To this day, it's worked. I don't want to feel the way I did after I acted like a jerk, and I want my kids to have great memories of me. I thought, became angry, acted ungodly, felt remorse, and began to think about how I was feeling. Since then my thinking has led to positive feelings and healthy responses, which in turn have led to a feeling of satisfaction and good thoughts about how I handled difficult situations. The result? A different family attitude and atmosphere.

Recommit

Those who respond appropriately to God's conviction have a shift in desire. Here's an important truth. Desire moves us in specific directions. Before we move, we face the direction we want to travel. If we desire the things of the world, we face the world, move toward the world, and take on the image of the world. We become "wrong" because we direct our love inward. This shuts off our light for God. If we desire God, we face God, move toward God, and take on the image of God. We're right because we show love to others by serving them, which turns on our light. It all begins with our shift in direction. This shift in direction is called repentance. So what is repentance? The Scripture teaches us what it is in Acts 26:20. The Bible reads, "I preached that they should repent and turn to God and prove their repentance by their deeds." The repentance part is the turning part. Our desire compass changes. We shift from a desire for the world to a desire for God. Some may confuse repentance with actual movement in a certain direction. This isn't the case. The Scripture teaches us that we prove our repentance by our deeds. In other words, we prove that we have changed direction and that we have turned by the actions we perform. Our commitment has changed and we know it because of what we do. We do something specific. We confess. Confession and repentance go together.

The Scripture makes a great promise to us about confession. We read, "If we confess our sins, he is faithful and just and will forgive us our sins and purify us from all unrighteousness" (1 John 1:9). God promises us He'll forgive us when we confess, if we agree with Him that what we did was wrong. That's what true confession is. It acknowledges that we were facing and going the wrong way and that we took on the image of the world. At that moment, our commitment changes. Commitment comes from the heart. When our desires change, our commitment always changes. Now we're committed to do what's necessary to begin moving in the right direction. This leads us into the next activity we're to perform in the restoration process. We have rewound and recommitted. What's next?

Renew

The first activity we're to perform that begins to move us in the right direction is changing the information in our minds. We must refocus. Remember, what we think leads to what we feel, and what we feel leads to how we act. We have a problem when we rewind and we recommit, but do nothing to change the information that's in our mind about our past failures. If this information doesn't change, we'll continue to break the law. It's a mind game.

The Scripture teaches us to change the information in our minds. Let's look at what it says. Paul writes this in the book of Romans: "Do not conform any longer to the pattern of this world, but be transformed by the renewing of your mind" (Romans 12:2). I know this may sound a little weird, but why don't you point to your mind right now. The Bible tells us we're to renew it. Say out loud, "Renew it!" We do this when we put new information into our minds. Say this out loud: "I need to put new information into my mind." (You can stop pointing now). Paul wrote about this as he penned a letter to the church at Ephesus. He says, "You were taught, with regard to your former way of life, to put off your old self, which is being corrupted by its deceitful desires; to be made new in the attitude of your minds; and to put on the new self, created to be like God in true righteousness and holiness" (Ephesians 4:22-24). Point to your mind again. We're taught that we're made new in the attitude of our minds. Say, "I need a new attitude!" In order to live a new life and follow a new direction, we must change our thinking. We're to have a new attitude in our heads. How do we do this?

To teach this, let's take a look at yet another passage, this time in the book of James. He writes,

> Do not merely listen to the word, and so deceive
> yourselves. Do what it says. Anyone who listens to
> the word but does not do what it says is like a man
> who looks at his face in a mirror and, after looking
> at himself, goes away and immediately forgets what
> he looks like. But the man who looks intently into
> the perfect law that gives freedom, and continues to

do this, not forgetting what he has heard, but doing it—he will be blessed in what he does.

James 1:22-25

This teaches us that we can see our face in the mirror and forget what we look like. What does that mean? To answer that question, let's answer another question: What are we to see when we look in the mirror? This is great! Remember, we are created in the image of God, therefore, we should see we are the image of God when we see our reflection. If we forget we're the image of God, we forget we're to live up to His image—to reflect Him. We walk away, forget about what God expects, and begin to think about the world's expectations. We begin taking on the wrong image because we're facing and moving in the wrong direction. We live up to the world's expectations, and not God's. There must be a change, and it takes place in the mind. We need to remember who we are and live up to the image we were created to live up to. God gives us His Word to teach how we're to do just that. If we don't change the image in our minds, we'll continue to fail. That's just a fact. Let's learn why this is true.

God created our bodies with the ability to change the information we store in our minds. Scientists have discovered that there are neurons in our brains called "mirror neurons." Here's how they work: When a situation arises, we see it and form an opinion about what is happening in our minds. Our thinking causes us to feel a certain way which, in turn, leads us to act out consistently with our emotions. All of this is stored in our mirror neurons. Something really interesting happens. If a similar situation arises and we haven't done anything to change the information in those mirror neurons, we reflect the same emotions and behaviors as before. So the key to changing our behavior is to change what's stored in those neurons. We need to refocus our attention. After we rewind and see our failures, it's critical we put new information into our minds that will lead us to succeed. By doing so, we literally change our minds.

The process of changing our minds is called manifestation. To manifest is to see what will happen before it occurs. Not only do we see what will happen, we also imagine how we'll respond. Manifestation is all about our imagination. These visions of our future can be either positive or negative. We can tell which one we are practicing by noticing what's going on with our emotions. We've already learned that our feelings give away our thinking. So let's consider the two options—hope or discouragement.

As we've learned, both hope and discouragement deal with our view of the future. If we see our future as bright, we have hope. If we see our future as bleak, we are discouraged. Which one are you? Hope comes from positive manifestation and discouragement comes from negative manifestation. God longs for us to live with hope. Because of this, He's given us the ability to change our perception of the future by seeing ourselves act obediently when a similar situation arises.

There's something really interesting about our minds. They can't tell the difference between what's real and what is not. Let me illustrate it for you. Have you ever had a scary dream? Were you afraid? You emotionally responded to something because of what was happening in your mind. This occurred because you believed it was real when it wasn't.

I can't stand spiders. Let me say that again. *I cannot stand spiders!* I have a recurring dream which absolutely "freaks me out." I see a huge spider coming down from the ceiling making a path straight for my head. I start swatting my arms, trying to keep it away from me. I'm not talking about swatting in my dream. I start flinging my arms around because I believe this is really happening to me. My wife wakes up and isn't surprised to hear me tell her it's the spider dream. In the last spider dream I had, it was coming at me from the side of the bed. I'm a little concerned about where it's going to come from next. Although there really are no spiders, my mind believes otherwise and I become fearful and act out physically because of it.

There's something else that's intriguing about the mind. It can't distinguish between the past, the present, and the future. What we see with our minds, our minds believe is real at that moment. That's why we respond in the moment when we think about things, whether past, present, or future. We're dealing with the future, so check out this example:

Imagine that you have a job interview coming up in two days for your dream job. You interviewed for a similar position in another company about two months ago, but it didn't go well at all. You can't believe how badly it went. There were things coming out of your mouth that were just flat embarrassing. Every time you think about it, you get stressed out. It happened in the past, but you're having feelings in the present about what happened. Now you have another chance, but you can't stop dwelling on how poorly you performed before. When you envision the upcoming interview, you see yourself doing the exact same thing you did before. Anxiety sets in. It's something you're imagining in the future, but you're feeling emotions related to the event now.

So what's the problem? You haven't "changed your mind." You haven't replaced what's in your mirror neurons. The chances you'll have another interview meltdown are great. You can change this! Instead of just fixating on your past experience, put some new information in your mind. It's important to think about what happened before. This was one of the steps we learned earlier about rewinding and learning from our past experiences. You have to rewind. This is an important exercise that helps you determine what you did wrong. Learning requires understanding past mistakes and discovering what you should do to make corrections. Now that you've learned, imagine the interview in a different way.

Instead of seeing yourself act in the way you did before, imagine you behave in a positive way that will make a good impression for God. You see yourself doing a great job of exhibiting your skills and living up to what God created you to be. If you do this, the chances of your having a good interview go way, way up.

Let's get spiritual. We have to do the same thing when we make mistakes and disobey God. We rewind, notice our failure, take ownership of it, and learn the correct way to think and behave. Now imagine a similar situation before it happens and see yourself doing the right thing. Stop thinking about your bad behavior and start thinking about what Christ would do. See yourself acting like Him the next time you are tempted to fail. Your chance of making the right choice improves significantly. Knowing the right thing to do has everything to do with our not forgetting what God instructs us to do. We're to look to God's Word to gain instruction about how to think, feel, and act in order to reveal His image to others.

We've learned we are to be like Christ. We discover, through God's Word, how Jesus reflected God's image. God knew we needed a physical example of who He is. Jesus is that image. How awesome is that? We're to be conformed into His likeness. Paul gives instruction about this. He writes, "For those God foreknew he also predestined to be conformed to the likeness of his Son, that he might be the firstborn among many brothers. And those he predestined, he also called; those he called, he also justified; those he justified, he also glorified" (Romans 8:29-30). This has been God's calling for us all along. It's always been His plan for us to look like Christ. To do it, we need His mind. His thoughts need to be our own. These thoughts lead to Christ-like emotions, and Christ-like emotions lead us to perform Christ-like actions.

It's time for another personal story. I'm having a tough day today. Even as I write this, I'm making a personal decision to put something out of my mind and something new into my mind. This morning (it's the past, but very recent) I opened up an anonymous letter from someone who visited one of our services. My secretary normally screens these notes and keeps them away from me, but this one made it through. I'm pretty sure the person who wrote it is an older pastor. I make this assumption because of my excellent profiling skills (Ha! I've been watching too much C.S.I.).

Pastors love getting mail like this. We arrive on Monday and hope we have a stack waiting on our desk. Obviously, I'm not serious. We hate it! At least I hate it. People who write these notes are gutless and prove something about their spirituality through their unwillingness to speak personally to the one with whom they disagree.

I struggle with criticism in a big way. I know it's not right and, when I do struggle, it proves I'm not where God wants me to be. I'm measuring myself by the opinions of man and not God at those moments. Here's my problem. I'm a "dweller." It's really hard for me to get these things out of my mind. As I write this, I'm having a hard time letting go of the situation I just described to you. How's that for a confession?

The person who wrote this letter was basically criticizing my preaching style, saying I wasn't an expository speaker. He implied that I didn't study enough to be an expository speaker. This was really hard for me to read because I spend a lot of time studying and have always thought of myself as an "expositor." He also inferred that I didn't apply God's Word to life. I couldn't believe I was reading this because I put special effort into doing just that.

Here are my options:

- Option #1 – Think the guy is a jerk and forget about it.
- Option #2 – Think the guy is a jerk but believe everything he said and get down about it.
- Option #3 – Think the guy is a jerk but try to find any truth that may be present in what he wrote.
- Option #4 – Know this guy is loved by God but has a heart problem which needs to change. Also look for any truth in what he said to see if he has revealed any blind spots I may have that need to be addressed. Finally, learn from these past mistakes and make changes in a positive way that will help me in the future. Pretty long option, but a good one!

Notice the last option is the only one that doesn't consider the guy a jerk. I know this is the proper option, but I'm having a really hard time not labeling him as—you guessed it! If I keep these wrong thoughts in my mind, I'll just be bitter about the future, and I'll believe that every old visiting pastor is going to think the same thing about me. I may even project these assumptions on other people. If I change my thinking, I can see the truth in what was written, if there is any. I can also see myself obeying God through my speaking and not being concerned about how man perceives me, but only being concerned about how God sees me.

Let's move on!

Remember

We are to remember the Word of God. Now that we know we're to change our minds, we need to learn how to change it. One of the best ways is the "good in and garbage out" principle. You've probably heard the phrase "garbage in and garbage out." It really is true. If we take garbage into our minds, garbage (bad behavior) comes out of us. So let's change it to be more positive. If we take good information into our minds, then garbage goes out. This "good stuff" in our minds will lead to good behavior. The way to do this is to take in the right information. This will change our focus. One of my favorite verses reads, "Create in me a pure heart, O God, and renew a steadfast spirit within me" (Psalm 51:10). This is sweet! Did you catch the word "renew?" We just learned about it in the previous step toward restoration. When our heart becomes pure (through confession), we become steadfast in spirit through renewal. This occurs because we take in God's instruction. Our thoughts now concentrate on Him. The good comes in and we throw the garbage out.

Practicing spiritual disciplines helps us remember God and directs our minds toward Him. We don't forget about Him. We remember! Because we remember Him, we want to get to know Him even more. We want to learn to trust Him and find strength in Him. When we remember Him, we begin to do what's necessary to keep our minds on Him. Again, keeping our minds on Him is the answer to overcoming challenging situations. We need to add some elements to our lives to do this. Practicing these disciplines adds something in us. We:

- *Add Spiritual Fuel.* I'm a Harley guy. There's nothing like feeling the wind on your face as you ride down the road. I've learned something about my Harley. If there's no gas, it doesn't go. I know you're amazed at my vast wisdom once again! This is common sense. I speak from experience. Fuel allows the engine to run, which puts the bike in motion. Here's the deal—we have to know we need it.

Not too long ago, I went on a ride and immediately started having problems. I'd gotten only about a half mile from home when the bike started sputtering and jerking around. Tim started to freak out. I had purchased the bike new and only had it for a short time and couldn't believe I was already having problems. I pulled over on the side of the road and called home to let Jennifer know what was going on. I told her the problem and started worrying (it's my nature) about how I was going to get someone to come and pick up the bike. I told her I would call her back in a few minutes to let her know if I could figure out what was wrong. I tried and tried to get it to crank and couldn't. Then it hit me. *I wonder if it has enough gas.* There was a fuel switch on the bike that allows fuel from the reserve to flow. I flipped it and the bike went *vrooooom!* Relief! It would have been really embarrassing to have a tow truck come and take it to the Harley shop only to fill the tank.

We need to make sure we're full of spiritual fuel. People who are running on empty rely on their own strength to fix their problems. It doesn't work. We need God. Our trust must be in him. If we don't fuel up, we forget about Him and we begin sputtering. Before long, we're broken down and we don't realize that our problem has been a false belief in self sufficiency rather than a knowledge of our need for the true source of personal power.

To get going, we need to fill our spiritual fuel tanks. With what?- you ask! With knowledge. The more we learn about Him, the more full our tank becomes and the farther we can go. We also fill our tanks by talking to Him. The more we communicate with God, the more our tank is filled and the farther we can go. Both spiritual exercises require discipline, but it's worth it. There's something else that should be added. We need to:

- *Add Accountability.* We need people around us who can help us. Paul wrote these words, "Brothers, if someone is caught in a sin, you who are spiritual should restore him gently. But watch yourself, or you also may be tempted. Carry each other's burdens, and in this way you will fulfill the law of Christ." (Galatians 6:1-2). Did you catch the last part of this verse? We are to carry other's burdens. We fulfill the law of Christ when we do. Do you remember the law? It's to love our neighbor. If we don't do this, we aren't fulfilling the law of Christ.

Having an accountability partner, someone we can be transparent with, helps us stay on course. An accountability partner meets some specific requirements. They:

o   know our failures (what we did wrong)
o   know our struggles (why we did it)
o   know our current thoughts and behaviors (where our thoughts are taking us)
o   speak the truth to us in love (they keep us on track by telling us what we need to hear, not necessarily what we want to hear).

If you don't have someone like this, you need someone like this. Get one now! Finally we are to:

• *Add Community.* A community is a group of people whom you hang with. This isn't just any community, it's a Christian community. Although attending a worship service is a community experience and focuses our minds on God, it's a really big community. We need a smaller group of people who know our names and care about our spiritual journey. This also gives us a place of service and ministry, a way to love our neighbor. I've learned that one of the greatest things that keeps us moving toward God is service. Ministry is the ultimate because we reveal the image of God when we serve. Service jacks us up! It gets us excited about our faith. It keeps our spiritual energy flowing. We need a place where this can happen. If you aren't in a small group, get in one now! I sound a little bossy, don't I?

If you're broken and struggling with your feelings, know this—God wants to restore you. Restoration requires you to act. So act!

God,
Thank You for Your truth. Thank You for revealing to me how I can be restored. I ask You now to help me as I renew my mind. Empty me of my selfish desires and fill me with Your Spirit. I long to please You.

Chapter Five

The "I'm Better Than You" Syndrome: Overcoming Pride

When pride comes, then comes disgrace, but with humility comes wisdom.

Proverbs 11:2

He thought he was "all that!" Who? Many have heard of Edwin Hubble. The Hubble Space Telescope was named after this famous astronomer. In his book, *A Short History of Nearly Everything*, Bill Bryson wrote about his life. He pointed out that Hubble was known for his athletic ability and his good looks. Although these strengths brought him attention, he's best known for his "smarts." You know, his intelligence. He studied physics and astronomy at the University of Chicago and was selected to be one of the first Rhodes scholars at Oxford. In a paper he wrote in 1924, he proved that the universe contained many galaxies. Until this time, astronomers believed there was one galaxy known as the Milky Way. He also proved the universe continues to expand through his research. This was another "huge" discovery.

Hubble has a place in history because of his amazing achievements, yet these accomplishments weren't enough for him. He exaggerated the truth about other experiences. Here are some examples: He claimed that he spent his late twenties and early thirties as a lawyer in Kentucky. He was a high school teacher in Indiana during that time. He bragged about events that happened during his life as a soldier during World War I, making people think he was a hero on the battlefield. The fact was he most likely never even heard gunfire. He spoke of a time when he daringly saved some drowning swimmers. Never happened! He also talked about fighting in an exhibition boxing match with a famous boxer, knocking him down. A figment of his imagination! This also never occurred.[14]

If Hubble were alive today, my question would be "Why?" Why did he stretch the truth? Why do any of us stretch the truth? Why do we lie? There are two reasons. We lie for self-protection or self-promotion. These moments in Hubble's life didn't represent times of needed protection; instead, they were opportunities to bring attention to himself. He was in "ego mode." This is pride.

Pink Pants and Pride

Pink pants have a way of breaking your pride. You're probably wondering what in the world I'm talking about. I had just entered high school and I was on the ninth grade football team. I wasn't a starter; in fact, I wasn't even on the second team. I was third string. Think about it. There is no lower position in high school football than ninth grade third string. Even though I was the lowest on the totem pole, I loved wearing my jersey to school on game day. I had an extra strut in my step, thinking I was somebody. It even got me out of having to dress down in P.E. and participate in whatever "life-changing" physical activity was scheduled for that day. After all, I had to rest up so I could play in the game. The chances of this happening were low—I mean really low. I had hoped when I signed up for the team that I would play more than three plays. Yep! An entire season and I was in a game for three plays. However, I did make a tackle that saved a touchdown. I think we were winning by about forty points. It was the only way the coach felt safe putting me in. The story continues!

If my low position on the team didn't humble me enough, then what I'm about to share with you did. It all had to do with a load of wash. My mom, who I love very much, put something red in with my white football paints and, you guessed it, the result was pink pants. I had no other pair and I was stuck. Mom tried to make me feel better about it, but I could tell she was about to burst out laughing. Can you imagine my horror, knowing I would have to stand on the sidelines in my pink pants with the rest of the team? On that day, I was glad not to get in the game. I'm sure I would have struck much fear in the eyes of the opponent with my stylin' "sweet" uniform. I hate to think about what the other team would have done to me. I can hear them now—"Hey, let's kill the guy with the pink pants!"

It was humiliating! I'd been trying to get attention from others in what I thought was an impressive way, and now I was getting attention in an embarrassing way. So much for my effort to get people to think I was something special because of my position on the football team. Now I was just a really bad dresser standing on the sidelines. Hello pink pants, so long pride.

I wanted to play in the game, but what I've learned about pride is that it happens in those who see life as a game. They have a competitive nature, and the winner is the one who receives the most attention. They use all of their energy to achieve this goal, even if it means harming others to prove their own self-worth. When pride defines us, it also directs us. It sends us on a course away from God. The desire of God is for humanity to see His love through us, a love which is defined by sacrifice—an act of selfless service. The prideful miss the mark. They reveal a love for self, using others as pawns in order to feel more valuable.

Pride wreaks havoc in relationships. It's a relationship killer. The prideful see people only as a means to an end. They believe in their own importance and that others are beneath them. They also believe they are always right and will do whatever it takes to prove it, even if it means bringing harm to someone else.

Pride influences us in another way. It affects our belief about our need for God. The prideful push God aside and make themselves ruler. I love the definition of pride given by Mary Kassian in her book, *Conversation Peace*. She defines pride as "focusing on my own rights, ability, or insufficiency instead of on God's glory, grace, and all-sufficiency.[15] This is a great definition because it relates our pride to how we see ourselves and how we view God.

It's easy to fall into the pride trap, and God knows it. That's why He warned the people of Israel of the consequences that would come if their hearts turned prideful, drifting away from Him. We read this warning in the book of Deuteronomy. God was preparing the people of Israel to enter into the Promised Land. Moses used this occasion to remind them about what God had done to bring them to this place. He also gave a warning, telling them what would happen if they forgot God. The warning involved pride. Take a look at his words:

> He humbled you, causing you to hunger and then feeding you with manna, which neither you nor your fathers had known, to teach you that man does not live on bread alone but on every word that comes from the mouth of the LORD.... Observe the commands of the

LORD your God, walking in his ways and revering him.... When you have eaten and are satisfied, praise the LORD your God for the good land he has given you. Be careful that you do not forget the LORD your God, failing to observe his commands, his laws and his decrees that I am giving you this day. Otherwise, when you eat and are satisfied, when you build fine houses and settle down, and when your herds and flocks grow large and your silver and gold increase and all you have is multiplied, then your heart will become proud and you will forget the LORD your God, who brought you out of Egypt, out of the land of slavery.

Deuteronomy 8:3, 6, 10-14, 17-18

What awesome instruction! We learn so much. If I am to overcome pride, I must first understand the symptoms of pride. There are several.

The Symptoms of Pride

What condition are we in if we are prideful? What's going on in our lives? What are the symptoms? We behave in certain ways when we are prideful. Let's check them out:

We Brag

Jeremiah writes, "This is what the LORD says: "Let not the wise man boast of his wisdom or the strong man boast of his strength or the rich man boast of his riches, but let him who boasts boast about this: that he understands and knows me, that I am the LORD, who exercises kindness, justice and righteousness on earth, for in these I delight," declares the LORD" (Jeremiah 9:23-24). God is the one who gave it all to us. It's about Him, not me. I need to answer a question—"Am I bragging about God or myself?"

Our life is about fulfilling His purpose for us. Our purpose is to help others reach their full potential. The Bible tells us, "For we are God's workmanship, created in Christ Jesus to do good works, which God prepared in advance for us to do" (Ephesians 2:10). Doing our good work is our act of humility. It builds God's kingdom, not ours. Problems come when we forget the role God has played in our development. Pride takes over and we believe we're self-made. We call attention to our actions and away from God.

Studio 60 on the Sunset Strip is a television drama about the life of the actors and crew who put on a show similar to *Saturday Night Live*. One of the main characters, Danny (Bradley Whitford), is an executive producer. He falls in love with the president of the network, Jordan (Amanda Peet), who is pregnant with another man's child. (The more I write about this, the more it sounds more like a nighttime soap opera). She goes to the hospital because she can't feel the baby move. One medical problem leads to another and she begins having seizures and bleeding internally. Her blood won't clot and she's in critical condition. They take the baby out by C-section and the baby is healthy; however, things don't look good for Jordan. Enter another character! Her name is Harriett (Sarah Paulson). She's one of the stage actors who is a born-again Christian. Throughout the show, she's challenged about her beliefs by a mostly non-religious group of people responsible for the weekly telecast. Here she is now with Danny, someone who doesn't believe in God, at the hospital waiting for word of Jordan's condition. Harriett, trying to encourage Danny, tells him she can do one of two things, she can do her Holly Hunter impression or she can teach him how to pray. He chooses to learn how to pray. Off to the hospital chapel they go. While there, Harriett gets on her knees and prepares to pray for Jordan when Danny says,

"I wasn't handed anything on a silver platter. I'm who I am because my parents gave me opportunities. I am who I am because I worked hard and got good grades. Because I went after a non-paying entry level internship to prove myself. I got what I got because I took action."

Harriett gives an awesome response.

She asks, "Are you a surgeon? Hematologist?

He responds, "No."

She asks, "Then what action can you take now?"

Wow! That really puts things into perspective for us, doesn't it? In pride we think we can control our own destiny when, in fact, we need others. It humbles us when we realize this. Pride gives us no hope, but faith in others can give us hope.

We Fight

The prideful attack others. They do this because they have to protect their territory. Solomon teaches us that "pride only breeds quarrels..." (Proverbs 13:10). He also writes, "The proud and arrogant man—'Mocker' is his name; he behaves with overweening pride" (Proverbs 21:24). You don't want to be known as an "overweener," do you? I think I just coined a new word!

Mocking is an aggressive behavior which leads to quarrels. When we mock, we're treating others with ridicule or contempt. We belittle other people to make ourselves look better. Kassian writes that "pride causes us to assume a battle posture."[16] We believe we must protect our position, so the gloves come out. The battle is on!

Pastor and author Max Lucado, in his book *A Love Worth Giving*, shares about the pecking order. He writes,

Have you ever heard the phrase "pecking order." We can thank Norwegian naturalists for the term. They

71

studied the barnyard caste system. By counting the number of times chickens give and receive pecks, we can discern a chain of command. The alpha bird does most of the pecking, and the omega bird gets pecked. The rest of the chickens are somewhere in between. The problem with the pecking orders is not the order. The problem is with the pecking. It's aggressive behavior. It's done to beat the other down to maintain position. Love has no place for pecking orders.[17]

The Pharisees had a pecking order problem. Jesus spoke to them about this attitude. They were concerned about maintaining their position before men: "Everything they do is done for men to see: They make their phylacteries wide and the tassels on their garments long; they love the place of honor at banquets and the most important seats in the synagogues; they love to be greeted in the marketplaces and to have men call them 'Rabbi'" (Matthew 23:5-7). The Pharisees felt threatened by Jesus. That's why they acted out aggressively against Him, leading to His death. They did this to protect their position, which is typical prideful behavior.

The actions of the proud bring about strife. God doesn't want this. It's contrary to God's plan for us. Paul emphasizes this in his letter to the church at Rome. He writes, "Live in harmony with one another. Do not be proud, but be willing to associate with people of low position. Do not be conceited" (Romans 12:16). It's a "harmony killer!"

We Don't Take Advice

Solomon taught us that "pride only breeds quarrels, but wisdom is found in those who take advice." (Proverbs 13:10). We make an assumption. The assumption is that we perfectly understand the situation when we really don't. We assume we don't need anyone else to help us make good judgments. Our refusal to be corrected can have some pretty dire consequences.

Ken Mercer, a writer for the *Mercer Island Report*, wrote an article about the prideful behavior of an airline pilot. Before Varig Airlines Flight 254 took off on September 3, 1989, the captain of the aircraft consulted the computer flight plan to determine the heading for their journey from Maraba to Balem. He mistakenly entered the wrong information in the computer navigating system. After takeoff, the plane turned west toward the Amazon forest rather than northeast toward the Brazilian coastline and their destination.

After several minutes, the captain sensed something was wrong and turned the plane around 180 degrees. The passengers began to wonder what was happening and sent word to the captain through the flight attendants. The captain lied and said there was a power failure at the Balem airport. He told them that they would circle the airport until the power was restored. Sixty-eight minutes later, at 7:39 p.m., the first officer discovered the mistake and attempted to explain it to the captain, but he refused to listen. Several minutes later, out of fuel, the pilot made a crash-landing in the forest. The plane was seven hundred miles off course. All six of the crew members survived, but thirteen of the forty-eight passengers were killed, all because a man in his pride refused to admit his mistake and be corrected.[18]

We need to be correctable, and we also need to have understanding. True understanding doesn't come from man's perspective, but from God's. If our understanding comes from man alone, we think in only physical terms. If we involve God, we begin to grasp the spiritual effects of our decisions. Kassian writes that "God is able to discern the thoughts and motivation of people's hearts. As we become more like Him, we become more apt to discern and understand. Our ability to understand people is, therefore, inseparably related to our relationship to God."[19] Paul got this. In talking about the one who teaches false doctrine, he writes, "He is conceited and understands nothing..." (1 Timothy 6:4). We need to take advice. Our refusal to do so leads to the next condition.

We Make Quick Decisions

Dude! Now it's getting really personal. Why? I struggle with this one. We react quickly and carelessly because we are overconfident about our ability to listen, interpret, and correctly respond to the other person. The Bible says, "Do you see a man who speaks in haste? There is more hope for a fool than for him" (Proverbs 29:20). We also read these words in James: "My dear brothers, take note of this: Everyone should be quick to listen, slow to speak and slow to become angry..." (James 1:19). We do the opposite if we make quick decisions. Believe me, I know! So what do we do during these times? We:

- Jump to conclusions.
- Don't control our tongues.
- Don't restrain our anger.

All of these lead to problems in our relationships and our ability to communicate the character of God to others through our behavior. To paraphrase, when we do these things, we have a hard time showing God's love. Isn't that what it's all about? We become the antithesis of what He longs for.

I mentioned earlier that I'm bipolar. Those who have this disease tend to either see things as better or worse than they really are. Now that I'm on medication, I'm much more able to recognize unrealistic expectations. However, before my diagnosis and treatment, I would often make quick decisions and not listen to advice, especially from my wife. This is already typical behavior from a man, so imagine how it was for me. Not a good situation, not at all!

It would be great if I could completely blame a chemical imbalance for all of my impulsive decisions, but I can't. Some of them simply come from pride. Even with meds, I must humble myself and be careful when making decisions. I have to daily focus my thoughts on the truth of God's Word, reminding myself I'm nothing without Him.

We've learned the symptoms, but what causes them?

The Causes of Pride

Pride doesn't happen on its own. There are influencers at work that cause its presence. Let's take a look at the issues that bring about this unhealthy emotion.

Arrogance

Do you know any arrogant people? Don't you just love hanging out with them? Of course not. Solomon writes, "to fear the LORD is to hate evil; I hate pride and arrogance..." (Proverbs 8:13). I can relate. I hate it in other people. But do I hate it in me? That's the question. The Scripture teaches us how we become arrogant. We can become arrogant when we forget what God has done (Deuteronomy 8:11-14).

The people of Israel were given very clear instruction; they were to remember what God had done. He had provided food for their survival, which was something the people were unable to do on their own. They needed God. Problems would come if they forgot. The prophet Hosea writes, "When I fed them, they were satisfied; when they were satisfied, they became proud; then they forgot me" (Hosea 13:6). Pride leads to forgetfulness.

We need to learn about a progression that occurs in life to better understand our pride. It's a vicious cycle. We move from one stage to another as we move toward trusting in God and away from trusting in ourselves. This is represented in the following diagram:

Trusting God Cycle

WE BELIEVE WE
DON'T NEED GOD

WE BECOME AWARE OF
OUR NEED FOR GOD

WE TRUST IN GOD TO
MEET OUR NEEDS

WE BECOME
SATISFIED

WE FORGET
GOD

WE FOCUS ON
PERSONAL SUCCESS
AND BECOME PRIDEFUL

- Step 1 – We believe we do not need God. This is a false belief of self-sufficiency.
- Step 2 – We become aware of our need for God. We discover we're not able to take care of all of our needs. We need help.
- Step 3 – We trust in God to meet our needs. This requires our faith. We know God is faithful because He's proven his love for us through sacrifice. We allow Him to rule over us. We make Him Lord.
- Step 4 – We are satisfied. We know God has met our needs and we experience joy that comes from being satisfied. This is a feeling of spiritual ecstasy.
- Step 5 – We forget God. Because we are satisfied, we easily forget why we are in this condition. We forget we need God.
- Step 6 – We focus on personal success and become prideful. We focus on our success. We begin to live for pleasure and not to please God. In pride, we stop looking at God and start looking at what we have. We redirect our trust.

Where are you in the cycle? Life becomes a merry-go-round when we keep going from one step of the cycle to the next. God doesn't want this to happen. We stop the cycle when we remember. We should never move past step four—being satisfied, knowing that God has met our needs. The meeting of our needs is a gracious act, one that is not deserved. We begin to focus on our success and become prideful, believing we no longer need Him, if we forget God and stop looking at Him.

The people of Israel were not to forget God; they were to revere Him (Deuteronomy 8:6). The people were to be thankful and follow God because of His loving actions. He was meeting their needs. Their remembering what God had done would result in reverence, which in turn, would result in their walking in His way. Forgetting what God had done would lead to irreverence. They would no longer walk in His way.

How does this happen? What causes us to forget and lose our reverence? The Scripture tells us we become distracted by success (Deuteronomy 8:13-14). God warned them about what could happen if they weren't careful. He told them they were going to be blessed with livestock and possessions. We read: "And when your herds and flocks grow large and your silver and gold increase and all you have is multiplied, then your heart will become proud and you will forget the LORD your God, who brought you out of Egypt, out of the land of slavery...." (Deuteronomy 8:13-14). They would become fixated on their abilities and possessions.

Survival

The survival instinct takes over when we don't feel loved. This reminds me of what happens to children who've been abandoned by their parents. Some believe that they're not loved and begin fending for themselves. They become very competitive, vying for the attention of others. They believe no one will meet their needs, and they begin feeling like they're on their own. They watch out for themselves. They become very selfish and begin taking pride in the fact they don't need anyone else. They are their own, God. Big mistake! I mean—really big mistake! Why? Because their life will implode when they realize they're incapable of meeting their own needs. What a sad state to be in. There is a third cause of pride.

Insecurity

The insecure find their value in how people perceive them. They begin drawing attention to themselves because of their need of acceptance. They have a value problem. They value the opinion of man more than the opinion of God. They feel successful only if they gain certain acceptance, recognition, or status. They begin promoting themselves in an effort to receive that acceptance, recognition, or status.

This reminds me of Hubble's life. It appears as though he was very insecure and felt the need to promote himself, even if it required lying. People do this because of insecurity and their desire to be seen as better than others. This goes directly against what the Bible teaches. Paul writes to the Church of Philippi, "Do nothing out of selfish ambition or vain conceit, but in humility consider others better than yourselves" (Philippians 2:3). Pretty clear teaching, wouldn't you agree? We have a huge problem when we falsely believe our value comes from being seen as better than others. Our value comes from the opposite. We are valuable when we help others become their best. It's not about us; it's about them. As long as it's about us, we let others lead us astray— causing us to experience unhealthy emotions and behaviors. It's when we realize our success comes from helping others become successful that we begin to find release from our insecurities. We are no longer insecure because we have a purpose. Let's learn more about how we can overcome our problem of pride.

The Prescription for Overcoming Pride

So how do we overcome our pride problem? There are two methods used to stop our pride. One is performed by God while the other is a personal choice.

Method #1 – Be Humbled

To be humbled, we must receive some tough love. God is the one who humbles us. He does this to change our thinking.

Remember, our emotions follow our thoughts. Think about the Israelites again. God performed some tough love on their journey to the Promised Land. The Scriptures teaches, "He humbled you, causing you to hunger and then feeding you with manna, which neither you nor your fathers had known, to teach you that man does not live on bread alone but on every word that comes from the mouth of the LORD...." (Deuteronomy 8:3). The people needed to learn they didn't know it all. They needed to learn of their great need for God. At times, so do we. This can be a really tough lesson to learn.

There's a wonderful truth taught in this passage. The truth is that what God gives, He can also take away. He can take away food to prove our need for Him. He can also take away our looks, possessions, health, and abilities. God has a way of reminding us who we are without Him. He humbles us for a reason. He does it to help us remember we really do need Him. The Bible says, "You may say to yourself, 'My power and the strength of my hands have produced this wealth for me.' But remember the LORD your God, for it is he who gives you the ability to produce wealth, and so confirms his covenant, which he swore to your forefathers, as it is today" (Deuteronomy 8:17-18). What's the second method?

Method #2 – Consider the Cause More Important Than the Credit

If I'm more concerned about the credit, I'm prideful. If I'm more concerned about the cause, I'm humble. The prideful can change their thinking by remembering that, as God's servants, we're to bring attention to who He is, not who we are. God may step in and intervene if we don't do this on our own. We lose our pride when we change our perspective of other people. Do you remember what Paul wrote? He gave the instruction to "do nothing out of selfish ambition or vain conceit, but in humility consider others better than yourselves" (Philippians 2:3). Our pride goes away when we consider others as better than ourselves.

Lucado told the story about Esther Kim, an aspiring athlete. For thirteen years she dreamed of competing in the Summer Olympics as a representative of the United States on the tae kwon do team. She began her training at the age of eight. During training, she met a girl named Kay Poe and they became best friends. Both were excited when they qualified for the 2000 Olympic trials in Colorado Springs. They were placed in the same division. This may sound like a good thing, but if they continued to win, they would have to face each other. Only one would be able to make the Olympic team. Something happened that made this situation even more challenging. Esther Kim was put in a really difficult position when Kay Poe injured her leg in a previous match. She could hardly walk, much less compete. Esther knew she now had the edge and that she could easily defeat her friend. This posed a big problem for her. She knew Kay Poe was the better fighter and, if she won the event, the best athlete wouldn't be going to the Olympics. There they were, ready for the competition, when Esther Kim stepped onto the floor and bowed to her friend. So what's the big deal? Sounds like just a nice gesture, right? It was much more than that. By bowing, Esther forfeited the match. Why? I love what Lucado writes—she "considered the cause to be more important than the credit."[20] Are those powerful words or what? Talk about humility! Here's the lesson: those who are humble don't care who gets the credit. They want to make sure the cause succeeds.

Are you showing symptoms of pride? You can wait for God to start the humbling process or you can remember God now and know the cause is more important than the credit.

God,
I confess my pride. I make the commitment to stop bragging and to start encouraging, to stop fighting and to start living in harmony, to stop refusing to take advice and to start listening to You, and to stop making quick choices and to start making right decisions. Your cause is worth it!

Chapter Six

Ticked or Tame: Overcoming Anger

"In your anger do not sin": Do not let the sun go down while you are still angry, and do not give the devil a foothold.

Ephesians 4:26-27

Put yourself in a time capsule right now and go back to the last moment you were "ticked off." You know, when you felt the wild angry beast in you come out and roar. Some don't have to go back very far at all—maybe fifteen minutes, an hour, three hours. What did it? What was it? Looking back, was it really worth it? Since I'm in the "asking questions" mood, let me ask you another one. If you could live that moment all over again, would you change your behavior or would you do it the same way?

One of the issues that influence us is called heartache. If our anger causes us heartache (pain), we want to change. If our anger causes heartache in someone we didn't want to hurt, we want to change. We wish we could yell "do over" like the kid on the playground who doesn't like the results of the game. Our game isn't going well, and yelling "do over" doesn't change a thing. It doesn't change our past. We do have a chance for a do over in the future, when a similar situation comes our way. We have a choice. Instead of being "ticked," we can be "tame." If we want to be "right" in those upcoming moments, we need to learn from what we did "wrong" in our past. Let's do it.

I think it's time for some more questions. What makes you angry? Where do you aim your anger? Do you direct it toward another person, yourself, or a situation? If you direct it toward a person, what do they do to deserve it?

Remember the progression we learned earlier about our emotions—we think, we feel, we act, we feel, and then we think again. Following this, we know our thoughts lead us to become angry. Something specific happens in our minds. We experience an unmet expectation. What we think should have happened didn't, and anger is the result. Think about expectations. These expectations are correct at times, while at others they're not. False expectations set us up for angry moments. Some even have false expectations about God. They become angry at Him when He doesn't come through in the way they expect. The solution is to correct their expectations.

False Expectations

There was a convicted murderer in a Romanian prison who obviously had an anger problem with God when he sued Him for his troubled life in October of 2005. He's known as Pavel M. The *Toronto Star* reported that he filed suit requesting "legal action against God, resident in heaven, and represented here by the Romanian Orthodox Church, for committing the following crimes: cheating, concealment, abuse against people's interest, taking bribes, and traffic of influence." Pavel made the accusation that "God even claimed and received from me various goods and prayers in exchange for forgiveness and the promise that I would be rid of problems and have a better life." According to the suit, God didn't meet this expectation and the plaintiff now found himself in the devil's hands. Can you believe that the complaint was sent to the Timisoara Court of Justice and forwarded to the prosecutor's office? The suit was dismissed because the defendant—God—was not an individual or a corporation, and therefore not subject to a civil court's jurisdiction.[21] Good thing. I was getting worried!

I'm struck by Pavel's comments because they illustrate what we've just learned. He had a false expectation of God. He thought that if He turned to God, then all of his problems would go away. God never promised our problems would go away. He did promise He would be with us as we face life's challenges. Pavel also indicated he believed that life is good when there are no problems. Once again, his mindset is completely wrong. A good life is not dependent upon our circumstances; a good life is dependent upon our relationship with God. Life is good because God, who loves us, is with us to encourage us at all times.

Is God meeting your expectations? Have you become angry at Him because He has not? People love to blame God for the things that go wrong. They do so because of their false expectations. They believe that God can be controlled. I know this may sound like a big claim, but think about it. They try to control God by living a certain lifestyle and, when they do, they expect God to bless them because of it. By the way, they have a definition of blessing—wealth and good health. You get the idea. The anger goes up when they lose money and their health goes south. They have the wrong idea of blessing. Here's the right idea. God being with us is a blessing. We can experience joy when the money goes or the body breaks down because God is with us.

Making Choices

If God isn't the cause of our problems, then who is? We've learned that we are created in His image. One of the defining characteristics of God is that He has the ability to make choices. We also have the ability to make choices because we are created in the image of God. God chooses for himself, not us, and we choose for ourselves, not God. Pretty cool, huh? Now we begin understanding why we have problems. We've made bad choices. That is, mankind has. Have you noticed that some of our problems are experienced because of our "bone headedness?" This means we had a "stupid" moment. We did something we knew we shouldn't have done, and now we're experiencing the consequences. At other times, we have problems because someone else made a bad choice that affects us. Here's some truth for you—God didn't choose these problems for us; we brought them on ourselves. But we blame God and get mad at Him. If I were Him, I'd be yelling, "That's not fair!" I'm not God, thankfully, but the statement is true. It isn't fair. We're blaming Him for something He has nothing to do with and we're messing up our emotions because of the lie in our minds. Satan is winning because he's successfully influencing us to put things in our heads that lead to our defeat.

Tim LaHaye and Bob Phillips taught this lesson in their book *Anger is a Choice*. They wrote about Norm Evans, who was an all-pro tackle for the Miami Dolphins for several years. He once said, "It's really dangerous for a pro football player to get angry. In fact, that's when linemen sustain their most serious injuries." He explained that "anger is so harmful in football that if I can get an opposing lineman or end angry at me, he will concentrate on beating me and forget to attack the quarterback—and that's my job, protecting the quarterback." They also wrote about Mike Fuller, a safety and punt-return specialist for the San Diego Chargers in the late '70s, who agreed with this statement. He said, "The wide receivers are continually trying to make us angry each time they come into our area, because they know if they can upset us emotionally, they can fool us on the next play."

If football doesn't speak to your heart, what about judo? They quoted Bob Hutchins, a former judo champion from Southern California who's now a missionary in Mexico. He said, "I was just an above-average judo performer until I learned how to make my opponent angry. Then I won the championship."[22] Our opponent wants to make us angry. His name is Satan. If he can influence us to choose to become angry, he can stop us from being a positive influence for God.

Just as we choose to become angry, we also choose how we are angry. You're probably wondering what that means. We choose to be right or wrong in our anger. Were you right or wrong the last time you became angry? Don't misunderstand my question. I'm not asking if your point of view was correct. Many times we become angry in relationships. We argue because we think we're right and we believe the other person is wrong. Anger may be a byproduct of the frustration we feel with people who don't agree with us. A better way to ask the question is—were you holy or unholy in your anger? Was God pleased with you?

It's possible to be holy in our anger. There are many passages in the Bible that tell us God was angry. For example, we read these words that describe God's emotional response toward the people of Israel:

> Then I said to you, "Do not be terrified; do not be afraid of them. The LORD your God, who is going before you, will fight for you, as he did for you in Egypt, before your very eyes, and in the desert. There you saw how the LORD your God carried you, as a father carries his son, all the way you went until you

reached this place." In spite of this, you did not trust in the LORD your God, who went ahead of you on your journey, in fire by night and in a cloud by day, to search out places for you to camp and to show you the way you should go. When the LORD heard what you said, he was angry and solemnly swore: "Not a man of this evil generation shall see the good land I swore to give your forefathers, except Caleb son of Jephunneh. He will see it, and I will give him and his descendants the land he set his feet on, because he followed the LORD wholeheartedly.

Deuteronomy 1:29-36

God became angry with the people because of their lack of trust in Him. Their behavior affected Him, and He responded emotionally. Did you get that? Man made a choice that affected God in a negative way. Wow!

Let's get back to His response. We know God is holy and cannot sin; therefore, we know His anger was correct in this situation. He became angry because of their unfaithful condition. He wanted them to improve. Holy anger is always used for a positive purpose, and that purpose is to make people better. It helps them; it doesn't harm them. Unholy anger is used for negative purposes and destroys others.

Paul gave instruction to the church at Ephesus about their emotions. He specifically refers to anger when he writes,

In your anger do not sin": Do not let the sun go down while you are still angry, and do not give the devil a foothold. He who has been stealing must steal no longer, but must work, doing something useful with his own hands, that he may have something to share with those in need. Do not let any unwholesome talk come out of your mouths, but only what is helpful for building others up according to their needs, that it may benefit those who listen. And do not grieve the Holy Spirit of God, with whom you were sealed for the day of redemption. Get rid of all bitterness, rage and anger, brawling and slander, along with every form of malice. Be kind and compassionate to one another, forgiving each other, just as in Christ God forgave you."

Ephesians 4:26-32

According to Paul, we can be angry and not sin. He also taught the reader to be careful about anger because the devil can gain a foothold if we allow anger to rule us. This happens when our beliefs are false. Satan is a liar and he wants to deceive us. Believing his lies results in our sinful anger.

The Silent Treatment

There are two primary ways we show our anger—aggressively or passive aggressively. Those who are aggressors are normally loud and can become physical, acting out against those who've ticked them off. The passive aggressor is the complete opposite. They're very quiet and retreat. I'm typically the passive aggressor.

No family is perfect. Is that an obvious statement or what? This is especially true of my family. We have times of agreement and times of disagreement. This isn't necessarily bad. It can be a good thing when our disagreements help us make better choices because of the perspective of others. However, it can be a really bad thing. This happens when one person has to win the conversation and be right.

I've mentioned that we have four children. They are really close in age and they have a tendency to want to be right, whether it's in a conversation with their parents or with one another. This is typical kid behavior. The problem is, when they want to prove they're right, they can get loud.

There's a reason for this and it goes back to the way my wife and I were raised.

I have two sisters, Teri, who is six years older than me, and Tina, who is four years older than me. There weren't many loud moments in my house growing up. We didn't frequently get in screaming matches with one another when wanting to prove our point. My two sisters and I had a great respect for our parents and normally kept things quiet. We didn't want the discipline that would come our way if we "got into it" with each other. I absolutely hate confrontation because I grew up in this environment. It drives me crazy to hear people argue with each other, and when I hear it, I get mad. I can't believe people would treat each other that way, and it makes me angry.

My childhood was much different than my wife's. There were four kids in her house, and like our children, they were also close in age. According to her, kids tend to be much more vocal with each other when this is the case. Jennifer and her brothers (David and Houston) and sister (Susan) also had great respect for their parents, but their communication style was very different. They were about the same age and would fight for the same things, and the result was "noise." It's not that it was bad; it was just different than what I experienced. The cool thing was they could argue and still like each other when the conversation ended. They'd be fine and move on.

Jennifer and I have brought two different cultures into our house because of the communication styles we were accustomed to from our childhoods. Because of the age dynamic of our children, guess which one wins out? You got it. The loud one! It drives me up the wall. Better put, it ticks me off. I can't stand coming home from work (which is quiet) and walking in the door to hear the volume immediately change. Let the arguing begin.

This isn't to bash my wife (by the way, she'll be approving all of the stuff in this book before you read it), but she frequently gets into the middle of the arguments with the kids and joins in. What's really interesting to me is she doesn't think she's arguing, nor do the kids. They just think they're having a conversation. Maybe they're right and I'm wrong, but I don't see it that way. I can't tell you how many times I've said to her and the kids, "Would you please stop arguing?" Do you know what they say? "We're not arguing!" It makes me mad, I put my mad face on (wrinkled forehead), and then I'm off to my room. I stay there and won't come out. When I do, I won't talk to the kids who got into the argument with Jennifer. I may not talk to them for a long time, depending on the tone of the conversation. I take it out on the kids because I assume they started it. I want them to pay. This is passive aggressive behavior. Please don't judge me, you messed up person! Yes, I called you a messed up person! We learned toward the beginning of the book that we're all "off." We're all at least one fry short. If you judge me, be careful, because I know you have your issues too. The good news is I know this about myself and I'm trying to deal with it. How can I get better? It goes back to something we've already learned.

The Activating Event

Earlier, we learned about the ABCs of our emotions. The "A" represents the activating event. The "B" represents our beliefs about the activating event. The "C" represents the consequence. We learned that our belief about the activating event is the determining factor in the consequences we experience. Anger is the consequence. We become angry because of our beliefs about a specific situation. We need to become aware of the beliefs that are leading us to act out in an unholy manner—whether aggressive or passive aggressive. We need to take a good look at ourselves and become aware of the effect our beliefs are having on us and others.

We can take action to find healing after we become aware of the cause of our unhealthy emotions. For example, the angry emotion I have over the arguing in my house may be coming from a wrong belief about these conversations. I believe my family members are angry with each other, when in fact they may only be expressing their opinion while having no animosity toward one another at all. If this is true, I need to change my belief so my behavior will also change.

A common belief is present when we act out in unholy anger in response to events. We believe we are the ones who matter most. Our emotions can be affected by the other defining areas of our lives, which include the physical, social, mental, and spiritual. We may feel threatened when we are angry in the following ways:

- **Physically** – believing someone wants to hurt "our bodies."
- **Socially** – believing "our position" in society is being challenged.
- **Mentally** – believing "our intellect" is being called into question.
- **Spiritually** – believing others disagree with "our view" of God.

Notice the word *our* in each statement from above. We respond in an unhealthy way when our concern is only for ourselves. We are consumed with how people treat us and we begin making demands on them.

David Augsburger, an expert in the area of relationships and confrontation, writes about this in his book, *Care Enough to Confront*. He states that "anger is a demand. Like, 'I demand an apology from you—an apology that suits me'... A demand that also demands others meet your demands."[23]

He writes that "freedom from being dominated by anger begins by tracking down the demands made on others.... Maturity comes through freeing others to live and grow without the imposition of controlling demands...."[24] He also emphasizes why these demands are present. He teaches that "the demands emerge whenever I see you as rejecting me or foresee you as about to reject me as a person of worth."[25]

We begin living in fear—a fear of rejection. This fear causes great anxiety and leads us to act out in anger. Augsburger deals with this issue when he writes, "Anxiety is the primary emotion. It signals that a threat is received, a danger is perceived, or a devaluation has been 'subceived' (subconsciously received) in another's response to me. Anger is a secondary emotion. It signals that demands are being expressed toward the source of pain, hurt, or frustration."[26] These feelings can lead us to begin acting out against those whom we feel are diminishing our personal value. Why? Because we live in fear that we'll be devalued. These destructive behaviors are unhealthy and are indications that Satan has a foothold that must be broken.

Unhealthy Behaviors

Anger is connected with unhealthy behaviors that have a negative effect on us and our relationships. Paul listed anger with bitterness, rage, brawling, slander, and malice. Anger plays a role in each. Let's take a look at them in more detail.

Bitterness – Our Refusal to Let Go of the Past

Those who dwell on past events tend to hold those past events against others. This occurs because of our unwillingness to forgive. We don't forgive because we're more concerned about how their behavior affects us than how our behavior affects them. Satan effectively influences us to believe our value is dependent upon what people do and say to us. He leads us to look to people for our sense of importance. All of us are looking for value and importance. God has wired us in this way. That's why we all want to be loved. We experience value and importance when we are appreciated and loved. The myth is that our value and importance come from people—imperfect people. This is a dangerous belief to hold because people will always let us down. Haven't you found this to be true?

Bitterness is a sign we've been looking to people for our sense of worth. It comes from our anger over not being treated the way we feel we should be treated. We've learned that anger is an action against something. If we are unholy in our anger, we're acting out against someone who has mistreated us. Bitterness is often expressed through passive aggressive behavior. There may be no yelling or physical violence; however, there is sarcasm and control. We try to make people pay by not giving access to things under our control, things that would be of benefit to them.

Our value should come from God. He does appreciate us and love us. His love never fails (1 Corinthians 13:8). Those who look to God for their sense of value don't dwell on unkind behavior that is received; rather, they know destructive behavior is a symptom of an unhealthy and distorted heart. They become concerned about the heart condition of those who are acting out in harmful ways and begin spiritually medicating them by caring for them. Grace, giving people what they don't deserve, and mercy, not giving people what they do deserve, are the two forms of God's love that heal a sick heart.

Rage – Attacking Behavior Used to Destroy Those Who Have Brought Us Harm

We want to fight and inflict pain. It's payback time! Where bitterness is often seen through passive aggressive behavior, rage is always aggressive behavior marked by violence. Unfortunately, there seems to be an epidemic of violence in our society today. This behavior often occurs because of an emotional hijacking. Our emotional mind takes over and we don't think rationally. We immediately go into a "fight" reflex without thinking about the consequences of our behavior. This occurs because of our desire to protect ourselves at all costs. The person who is in a rage feels attacked and devalued and acts out to regain their value through force.

Those who have rage issues often have an unhealthy sense of self-importance. God did wire us to be valued and to know we are important. He created every human being in the same way. The person who acts in a rage may falsely believe they're more important than the person who's acting out against them. They try to take control through violent behavior to prove who's king. Rage is a sure sign God isn't king of their hearts, they are.

Before you say you don't have a problem with this, think about your driving habits. It's amazing how the sweetest little grandmother can become Satan behind a wheel when someone cuts her off. We get miffed because of what people do to us—sometimes inadvertently. Our road rage is a sure sign we believe life is all about us. By the way, if you're one of those people who act this way, you may want to make sure you don't have the Jesus fish on the back of your car. You might be giving people the wrong idea about the Christian life. Just a thought!

Brawling – Fighting for the Purpose of Maintaining Personal Position

When I think of brawling, I think of two people in a fist fight. It's flashback time. I've had one fight my entire life. It was in middle school with a guy who annoyed the stew out of me. Just a little southern lingo there. He had been bullying me for a while and I was getting sick of it. He wasn't your normal bully. He was small, like me, with a huge ego. He'd pick on me and pick on me. Finally, I had enough and I mouthed off to him, trying to get him to stop. The next thing I knew, he was telling me he'd meet me in the bathroom when the period was over. Guess what? I showed up. I was waiting for him when he came in. He started talkin' trash again. Then he reared back and threw a punch at my head. Don't get worried for me. It was like in the movies. Things seemed to be going in slow motion. I ducked, missing his fist, and threw a punch right to his midsection. It was my Rocky Balboa moment. He doubled over and the fight was over. It was a short but sweet brawl. I don't advocate this! Just a statement for those parents out there who might think I'm leading their kids astray.

This is obviously one form of brawling, but there is also another type—arguing. It's about who's right and who's wrong. Many people find their value in being right. You may know someone like this. Somehow, they feel belittled when they're wrong, so they hate to admit it. Some fight for an incorrect position far too long because of their unwillingness to "own up" to their mistake. They become angry when they're challenged about their position and begin lashing out at others to prove they're right.

Brawling is yet one more symptom of a selfish heart. There's a difference between standing up for what's right and standing up because you have to be right. Those who stand up for what's right do so with respect for others. Showing respect for God's creation is always right. Those who stand up to be right must be seen as better than others for their sense of worth. Life will always revolve around them. As long as their position is maintained, they're happy, but as soon as their position is challenged, they fight.

Slander – Unwholesome Talk Used to Belittle

Paul writes, "Do not let any unwholesome talk come out of your mouths, but only what is helpful for building others up according to their needs, that it may benefit those who listen" (Ephesians 4:29). The word *unwholesome* is really important in this verse. It contains the word *whole*. Unwholesome talk is used to keep someone from feeling complete. It's used to make them feel they're less of a person than the one making the critical or demeaning comments.

Slander is also a form of anger. The person slandering feels threatened and becomes angry and acts out verbally. Again, this happens to protect or promote oneself. James wrote, "The tongue also is a fire, a world of evil among the parts of the body. It corrupts the whole person, sets the whole course of his life on fire, and is itself set on fire by hell." (James 3:6). Here's the deal - our tongues are a reflection of our hearts. James also wrote, "With the tongue we praise our Lord and Father, and with it we curse men, who have been made in God's likeness" (James 3:9). If our hearts are right, we praise God. One way we praise God is by treating mankind, who is made in His likeness, with respect and love. Our words are used to build, not destroy. If our hearts are not right, we curse men. This is connected with the next unhealthy behavior.

Malice – Deliberate Action to Harm

Once again, our anger is seen through behavior that's used to destroy and not build. Our anger is seen through malice, which is often revealed in our spreading of rumors or through gossip. Those who spread rumors tell lies in order to destroy the reputation of someone with whom they are angry. Those who gossip speak the truth about someone, but they do it for a self-centered purpose. Those who spread rumors share information that is untrue in an effort to inflict pain on the one with whom they are angry. Typically, gossip and rumors are used to maintain our own status or position. This comes from a self-centered heart that has no regard for others.

Malice also comes in another form. It's action taken to harm others in a nonviolent way to get revenge. I read a wild story about a couple who was having serious problems that illustrates this. FoxNews.com reported about a heated marriage situation between Tim Shaw, a British radio host, and his wife, Hayley. Tim told a pin-up girl he was interviewing on air that he was willing to leave his wife and two kids for her. This didn't sit well with his wife. She soon after created an eBay auction for her husband's high-end car, a Lotus Espirit Turbo. The eBay page had a picture of the car with these words: "I need to get rid of this car immediately, ideally in the next 2-3 hours before my cheating (jerk) husband gets home to find it gone and all his belongings in the street. I am the registered owner and I have the registration. Please only buy if you can pick up tonight." The car was listed with a "Buy It Now" price of fifty pence (ninety cents). The auction lasted exactly five minutes and three seconds before an anonymous buyer paid for it and drove away. Hayley was later interviewed about what occurred and said she was "sick of (Tim) disrespecting this family for the sake of his act." When asked about the price of the car, she said, "I didn't care about the money. I just wanted to get him back." The anonymous buyer left the following feedback on Mrs. Shaw's eBay account four days after the car was sold: "Thank you, Hayley, the car is excellent. Thank your hubby for me."[27] They both acted deliberately and the consequence was great.

Something common comes from all of these unhealthy behaviors associated with anger. People are affected in a negative way through each of these behaviors. Their life isn't made better. They feel devalued because of angry action. We learned earlier that holy anger is shown for a positive purpose. These behaviors have only negative consequences. This is really sad, knowing that God wants to use us to help people feel valued and important. Paul writes, "But now you must rid yourselves of all such things as these: anger, rage, malice, slander, and filthy language from your lips" (Colossians 3:8). How do we rid ourselves of these destructive behaviors? We must behave ourselves.

Healthy Behaviors

I don't know how many times my mama told me to behave myself when I was going to a friend's house. This seems to be a common statement from parents. It must be in the parent handbook. Why do I say this? I don't know how many times I've said the same thing to my kids. We need to know what behaviors are expected if we are going to behave ourselves. The Scriptures teach us what they are. Paul writes, "Be kind and compassionate to one another, forgiving each other, just as in Christ God forgave you" (Ephesians 4:32). These behaviors are quite different from the unhealthy behaviors we've just learned. Let's get into the details of the right way to behave. We are to:

Be Kind – Treat People with Respect and Love

Kind behaviors are the opposite of unkind behaviors. Once again, my intelligence just blows me away sometimes. Common sense, right? The unhealthy behaviors from above are all unkind because they're used to devalue. Those who are kind add value. The kind:

- Aren't bitter, holding on to the past. They let go and purposefully live to make the world a better place.
- Don't act in a rage, violently acting out to punish others. They respond with calmness, knowing that the behavior of others reflects their hearts.
- Don't brawl, attempting to protect their position. They're used by God to show love and bring about peace.
- Don't slander, using their words to belittle. They use their words as a gift of encouragement.
- Don't show malice, spreading rumors and gossip. They say and do things to improve and protect someone's reputation.

Just a personal question—how would your life improve if you lived up to these definitions of kindness?

Be Compassionate – Have a Heart That Breaks Over the Unhealthy Heart Condition of Others

The compassionate care. They feel a sense of sadness over those who are living for wrong purposes. They know that those who act in unhealthy ways need to experience an inner healing that comes from finding a never-ending love that gives true value and worth.

How would your life improve if you became compassionate?

Be Forgiving – This Is the Indication That We Love Like Christ Loves

We're to forgive as Christ forgave us. The crucifixion took place because mankind acted aggressively toward Jesus. It's an amazing love that can forgive those who attempt to kill us. They didn't attempt to kill Jesus; they did kill Him. He spoke powerful words as He hung on the cross — "Father, forgive them, for they do not know what they are doing" (Luke 23:34). Jesus wasn't concentrating on their actions; He was focusing on their hearts. He knew they didn't comprehend what they were doing to Him. He knew they were trying to find their value from man and not God. Jesus threatened their position, so they hung Him on a cross to silence Him. His claims made them angry, and they acted against Him to prove they had power. They didn't realize they were living for the wrong purposes. Jesus saw the condition of their hearts, was kind and compassionate, and was able to forgive. He didn't hold their behavior against them; He pitied them. We forgive when we don't hold the behavior of the unkind against them. We stop looking at their actions and start understanding the false beliefs that led them to behave in an aggressive manner.

How about another story? Amy Biehl, a 26-year-old white Fulbright scholar, died a violent death in 1993. She was beaten to death by a group of black Africans who wanted to overthrow the apartheid government. She had been registering black voters for South Africa's first free election when she was dragged away and killed. Her parents responded in an amazing way. Linda and Peter Biehl established a foundation in their daughter's name, quit their jobs, and moved from California to South Africa. Today, two of their daughter's killers work for the foundation. Linda made this comment about her ability to work with these men. She said, "Forgiving is looking at ourselves and saying, 'I don't want to go through life feeling hateful and revengeful, because that's not going to do me any good.' We took Amy's lead. We did what we felt she would want."[28] Amy's parents were able to see the people and stop looking at their behavior. Isn't that exactly what Jesus did? This allowed them to impact murderers. These murderers had a change of heart and became people who made a difference. Do you get it? Forgiveness has the power to defuse anger and transform a person's heart.

The "Sun Down" Principle

We've been learning about the devil having a foothold through anger as we respond inappropriately through unhealthy behaviors. He can also gain a foothold if we let the sun go down on our anger. That's what the Scripture teaches us. We read, "…Do not let the sun go down while you are still angry, and do not give the devil a foothold" (Ephesians 4:26-27). What does this mean? We're not to go to bed angry. I've heard this advice given to married couples many times over my life, and I can say with certainty, as someone who has been married for twenty years, that it's an awesome instruction. It really is possible to follow this principle (sometimes it's really hard).

Here's what we learn from the Scripture. God didn't intend for anger to be long-lasting. Aren't you glad God doesn't allow His own anger to linger? The Psalmist writes, "For his anger lasts only a moment, but his favor lasts a lifetime…" (Psalm 30:5). We also read, "The LORD is compassionate and gracious, slow to anger, abounding in love. He will not always accuse, nor will he harbor his anger forever…" (Psalm 103:8-9). We need to "get godly" and live like Him. To be like Him, we have to let things go.

Why should we follow this advice? The answer is pretty simple. Unresolved issues fester and lead into destructive behaviors. This isn't a healthy situation. If we don't resolve our beliefs about the events that have led to our anger, bitterness will set in. Bitterness can grow into other forms of unholy anger which place demands on other people, devaluing them.

Righteous Anger

We learned that we sin in our anger when we place demands on others to meet our own demands. The key to not sinning in our anger is to stop placing demands on other people and to start protecting them by ensuring they feel important. This happens by our showing God's love through sacrifice and service. Let's learn about righteous anger.

Righteous Anger Is an Anger That Stands Up for Other People

Do you remember this story about Jesus' life? He went to the temple and people were selling stuff, not for a righteous reason, but to fill their pockets. Jesus got mad, and I mean really mad. The Bible says,

> Jesus entered the temple area and drove out all who were buying and selling there. He overturned the tables of the money changers and the benches of those selling doves. "It is written," he said to them, "'My house will be called a house of prayer,' but you are making it a 'den of robbers.'"
> Matthew 21:12-13

The temple was to be a place where people could come and show their love for God by praying to Him. It was to be a house of prayer. Jesus became angry because the people were not valuing God. The moneychangers also had another issue. They were devaluing the people by taking advantage of them financially. This also angered Jesus. We should become angry when people are taking advantage of others for personal gain. It goes against what God created us to be—servants. This leads us to another lesson.

Righteous Anger Is an Anger Aimed at Behavior, Not at People

I've often heard the statement that we are to hate sin and love the sinner. It's true! This is also true with regard to anger. Our anger should be aimed at evil behavior, not at the person. Those who aim their anger at the person use destructive language, while those who aim their anger at the behavior use encouraging language that can change a heart. They concentrate their words on the behavior that is self-destructive.

I'm human just like you. It's tough to aim our anger in the right location. In the past, I've found myself talking about what other people have done to harm me. My anger in those moments was directed toward the person, not the behavior. It was payback time. I wanted them to pay for what they had done to me. Unhealthy behaviors were the result. I've found that when I become less concerned about what people are doing to me and more concerned about what they are doing to themselves, it changes how I speak to them. I speak in a way that expresses concern for their condition. I find myself asking them about the events in their lives and what they believe about those events that have led them to behave in a destructive way. My goal is to help change their false beliefs and see the truth about our true source of value. There is a final lesson.

Righteous Anger Occurs When My Thoughts Are Right

This brings us back to the words Paul uses to encourage believers. He writes, "Finally, brothers, whatever is true, whatever is noble, whatever is right, whatever is pure, whatever is lovely, whatever is admirable — if anything is excellent or praiseworthy — think about such things" (Philippians 4:8). We've learned that anger follows our beliefs. If we believe what is false, it causes anxiety, which leads to unrighteous anger. If we believe what is correct, we behave ourselves. We know we will respond with the right anger when we think about what is:

- True – What does God want?
- Noble – How can I show God's love?
- Right – How can I protect others?
- Pure – What should I do to protect God's reputation?
- Lovely – How can I serve to encourage a change of heart?
- Admirable – What sacrifices should I make to give evidence of God's love?
- Praiseworthy – What can I say and do that will lead people to trust in God?

Are you right or wrong in your anger? Right anger influences people toward positive change and causes them to see God. Wrong anger destroys. Behave yourself!

God,
I ask You to help me find my value from You. If I have been angry, I ask You to help me focus on people and stop fixating on their behavior. I also ask You to help me have a mind that thinks about what is true, noble, right, pure, lovely, admirable, and praiseworthy. May

my emotions and behaviors always have a positive effect for Your kingdom.

Chapter Seven

I Want It Too!
Overcoming Jealousy

Anger is cruel and fury overwhelming, but who can
stand before jealousy?

Proverbs 27:4

One of my favorite animated films is *Toy Story*. The
movie is about a boy who has a room full of toys. His
favorite is Woody, a cowboy. Woody loves him and enjoys
being the favorite toy. You know this because, of course,
the toys can talk to each other when he's not in the room.
This makes me wonder about my toys during my childhood!
Anyway, back to the story. Things get a little crazy when
a new toy is given to the boy for his birthday. His name is
Buzz Lightyear. He has a laser light, wings, a spacesuit, and
he claims he can fly, unlike Woody, who's getting older and
beginning to wear out. Woody's emotions get the best of
him, and the fun begins! Watch it. I think you'll like it.

This may seem a little ridiculous because it's a cartoon,
but the feeling Woody has in the movie isn't unusual at all.
It's real. It's the feeling of jealousy. If not dealt with in the
right way, we find ourselves going down a rocky emotional
road. So where does it come from? Great question! We begin

having this feeling when we want what others have. This feeling stems from a spiritual issue—love. If I have a jealousy problem, I have a love problem. I have a love problem when I don't love others enough. In other words, I love me more than I love them. I can't be excited for others because of what they have; I must have it too. Here's why. My worth isn't dependent on who I am as a creation of God; my worth is dependent on worldly measurements. I begin measuring myself against other people, which eventually leads to great disappointment. We experience emotional breakdown. How do we change this behavior?

We see an example in the Bible of some guys who became very jealous of their brother. His name was Joseph. Let's take a look at the story:

> Now Israel loved Joseph more than any of his other sons, because he had been born to him in his old age; and he made a richly ornamented robe for him. When his brothers saw that their father loved him more than any of them, they hated him and could not speak a kind word to him. Joseph had a dream, and when he told it to his brothers, they hated him all the more. He said to them, "Listen to this dream I had: We were binding sheaves of grain out in the field when suddenly my sheaf rose and stood upright, while your sheaves gathered around mine and bowed down to it." His brothers said to him, "Do you intend to reign over us? Will you actually rule us?" And they hated him all the more because of his dream and what he had said. Then he had another dream, and he told it to his brothers. "Listen," he said, "I had another dream, and this time the sun and moon and eleven stars were bowing down to me." When he told his father as well as his brothers, his father rebuked him and said, "What is this dream you had?

Will your mother and I and your brothers actually come and bow down to the ground before you?" His brothers were jealous of him, but his father kept the matter in mind.
Genesis 37:3-11

The brothers were envious of what Joseph had. He had their father's attention, and they wanted it! They were reminded of this each time they saw the coat of many colors. That wasn't the only problem. Joseph was a gifted guy and had the potential to become a great leader. They were reminded of this by Joseph himself. He was quick to tell them about his dreams and shared with them the interpretation of those dreams—that he would one day rule over them. Their jealousy got the best of them and they acted out in anger. That's what happens when we become jealous. This feeling becomes the catalyst for our self-protecting and self-promoting behavior.

The Categories of Jealousy

Jealousy falls into one of two categories—Type "A" or Type "B."

Type "A" Jealousy – The State of Being Wary of Being Replaced and Losing the Affection of Another

This jealousy describes God's jealousy. There are several Scriptures in the Bible that tell us God is a jealous God. God cannot sin; therefore, there must be a type of jealousy that isn't sin. This is it! We see an example of this in the book of Deuteronomy. God was having a problem with the people of Israel. The Bible says, "They made him jealous with their foreign gods and angered him with their detestable idols" (Deuteronomy 32:16).

The people had turned their backs on their relationship with God and directed their love to another object of worship. Israel, God's chosen people, had declared their commitment to Him, but they abandoned Him and loved another. God's jealousy is righteous because it comes from His feeling toward their behavior, a behavior that was wrong. Did you notice what you just read? His jealousy was aimed at their "behavior." He was concerned about their failure.

This reminds me of the relationship between husband and wife. I'm a jealous husband. I can promise you that if my wife cheated on me, it would bother me. She has declared her love and her life to me. I believe my wife is glad I'm a jealous husband. If you're married, don't you want to know it would bother your spouse if you cheated on them? Of course you do! This jealousy is an indication of their love for you.

Righteous jealousy centers on what is real and not on what is imagined. Some spouses become jealous over things that aren't true. This emotion comes out of a fear of what might happen, not what is really taking place. Those who experience this become paranoid about their spouse cheating on them and begin acting out in an unhealthy way. This destroys relationships because their jealousy becomes sin. There's no reason to lose trust, but they no longer have faith in the one who's made a commitment to them. Because of this, they become controlling. Ironically, many people who become controlling push their spouse away, resulting in their looking for affection from another. There's also another type of jealousy.

Type "B" Jealousy – The State of Being Envious, Resulting in Our Becoming Resentful or Bitter, Causing Us to Begin a Rivalry

This is unrighteous jealousy. The feeling doesn't come from a concern for another's failure, but from a concern for how someone else is affecting us. The Bible says,

> But if you harbor bitter envy and selfish ambition in your hearts, do not boast about it or deny the truth. Such "wisdom" does not come down from heaven but is earthly, unspiritual, of the devil. For where you have envy and selfish ambition, there you find disorder and every evil practice.
> James 3:14-16

The devil has a foothold in our lives, and our envy causes us to act out in evil ways. Notice that "bitter envy" and "selfish ambition" are connected. Our bitter envy comes from our own selfish ambition. We want what we want and no longer care about what others need. They need us! They need our love!

The Causes of Type "B" Jealousy

There are three causes of this type of jealousy. It's important to know the causes so we can prepare our minds to make good decisions when these situations arise. Remember, what we do with our rational mind during non-stressful times prepares us for the challenging moments of life.

Cause #1 – Our Inability to Be Happy for the Success of Others

There's an old fable told about two shopkeepers who were bitter rivals and didn't want the other to succeed. Their stores were directly across the street from each other. They would spend each day keeping track of each other's business. If one got a customer, he would smile because he felt superior to his rival. One night an angel appeared to one of the shopkeepers in a dream and said, "I'll give you anything you ask, but whatever you receive, your competitor will receive twice as much. Would you be rich? You can be very rich, but he will be twice as wealthy. Do you wish to live a long and healthy life? You can, but his life will be longer and healthier. What is your desire?" The man frowned, thought for a moment, and then said, "Here is my request: Strike me blind in one eye!"[29]

I'd say the dude in this story had a real problem. What about you? He wanted the other one to hurt so much that he was willing to experience pain himself to make sure the other was harmed even more. How would you like to have this guy for a friend? It's really sad when we are unable to be happy for the success of another because of our selfish hearts. We become concerned that others are succeeding and we're not. Shouldn't it be a good thing that people are succeeding, even if they're more successful than we are? As believers, we should be happy for their success.

Cause #2 – Our Feelings of Inadequacy

Those who feel inadequate feel like they've been short-changed. They feel like they aren't as blessed as someone else because they don't look as good, don't have as much as them, or are not as talented as their rival. The movie *Amadeus* is a great example of this. It's a story of how jealousy can consume us. Antonio Salieri and Wolfgang Amadeus were both pianists and composers. Antonio became very bitter over Wolfgang's amazing musical talents. He became very famous and was the center of attention in the musical world. This angered Antonio even more. Wolfgang died, and when this occurred, Antonio celebrated, believing his life would now somehow be better. This was not the case, not at all. At the end of the movie, Salieri is sitting in an insane asylum, cursing God. He's angry with Him because He didn't give him the same level of ability as Mozart.

How sad! He was overcome with so much bitterness that he couldn't see he was fearfully and wonderfully made. The Psalmist writes, "I praise you because I am fearfully and wonderfully made..." (Psalm 139:14). You and I are not less valuable because we don't look as good or have as much as someone else. We need to find our value from what God created us to be. If we don't, we distrust God and start trusting ourselves to do something about how people see us. This leads to the third cause of this type of jealousy.

Cause #3 – Our Comparing Ourselves to Other People

Some compare themselves to the people who are plastered on TV, in the movies, and in magazines, and they allow them to be their measurement for success. Again, what God created us to be should be our measurement. Maybe you don't struggle with trying to become like your favorite movie star. It's possible you still struggle with jealousy. In his book, *Status Anxiety*, Alain de Botton writes, "Given the vast inequalities we are daily confronted with, the most notable feature of envy may be that we manage not to envy everyone. We envy only those whom we feel ourselves to be like."[30] What a great perspective! Don't we do this? We find people who are similar and we compare ourselves to them.

We say something like this—"They shouldn't get the promotion because I'm as good as they are."

We tend to compare ourselves to those who are similar to us in three areas:

- **Recognition**. This is connected to our authority. People have recognized our worth and have given us a higher position of authority because of it. Saul fell victim to this. The Bible says, "As they danced, they sang: 'Saul has slain his thousands, and David his tens of thousands.' Saul was very angry; this refrain galled him. 'They have credited David with tens of thousands,' he thought, 'but me with only thousands. What more can he get but the kingdom?' And from that time on Saul kept a jealous eye on David" (1 Samuel 18:7-9). We buy into the lie from Satan that we're important only if we're more highly recognized. This is incorrect thinking. Our wrong belief brings about the wrong emotion of jealousy.

  I've struggled with this myself. You would think that in the ministry there would be no jealousy. Wrong! The Bible even teaches us this. We read, "It is true that some preach Christ out of envy and rivalry, but others out of goodwill" (Philippians 1:15). Ministers have a tendency to measure their success by how much bigger and better their church is compared to others. I know I have to fight these feelings. We put on a good face and tell pastors who are growing big churches that we are excited about what God is doing, when deep down inside we're stewing. We cop an attitude with God, wondering why He doesn't let us experience the same success. We know we've done this when the pastor we compare ourselves to has a moral failure and we can't wait to tell others about their fall. How sick is this? I know it's sick because

I've fallen into that trap before. The longer I'm in ministry, the more I realize that wherever God places us in ministry is an awesome place, no matter what size the church may be. Our success is not determined by big crowds; our success is dependent upon our service which leads to changed lives. I'm excited to say I don't struggle with this nearly as much as in the past. It feels good to be excited about what others are doing to make a difference for the kingdom.

- **Reward**. This is connected with our finances. We compare our cars, houses, and vacations. We begin coveting what our neighbors have. James writes, "What causes fights and quarrels among you? Don't they come from your desires that battle within you? You want something but don't get it. You kill and covet, but you cannot have what you want. You quarrel and fight. You do not have, because you do not ask God. When you ask, you do not receive, because you ask with wrong motives, that you may spend what you get on your pleasures" (James 4:1-3). We buy into the lie of Satan and believe our lives are better if we have more than the people we know. This wrong belief also leads to the wrong emotion of jealousy.

- **Relationships**. This is connected to our family and friends. We compare our circle of friends, our marriages, and our kids. Comparing kids seems to be a huge deal in our culture today. Not only do we put pressure on ourselves when we make these comparisons, but we also put pressure on our children to conform to a worldly standard. We buy into the lie from Satan that life is about having a family that's more successful by secular measurements than other families. This wrong belief leads to jealousy.

My wife is a former elementary school teacher. She runs the church's daycare and does a fabulous job. What a shameful way of trying to get on my wife's good side, right? She told me a story about something that happened while she was teaching in one of our public schools years ago. One of the kindergarten teachers had given the kids some worksheets to do as a learning project in class and sent them home after the end of the day. Before she gave them to the parents, she had drawn smiley faces on each of their worksheets as an encouragement. She had quickly done this so the kids could take the sheets home. The next day, one of the parents came by to see the teacher because her kindergartner hadn't received a full smiley face like other children. The parent had gone home and checked the worksheet, then looked at what the teacher had drawn and felt like her child deserved better. The next day the parent was in the teacher's room asking questions about why her child had received such a bad grade. The smiley face wasn't even a grade; it was just a nice gesture from the teacher to encourage the kids. She had drawn it quickly and, obviously, it didn't meet the criteria of proper smiley face drawing. Wow! No pressure for that kid!

Each of the areas of comparison from above can become a spiritual cancer that begins to grow and overtake us. It's sad when we begin to lose sight that we're fearfully and wonderfully made.

The Consequences of Type "B" Jealousy

Living with Type "B" jealousy affects us in several ways. There are consequences. They include:

Loneliness

Jealousy and envy are acts of a sinful nature. Paul writes, "The acts of the sinful nature are obvious: sexual immorality, impurity and debauchery; idolatry and witchcraft; hatred, discord, jealousy, fits of rage, selfish ambition, dissensions, factions and envy; drunkenness, orgies, and the like. I warn you, as I did before, that those who live like this will not inherit the kingdom of God" (Galatians 5:19-21). When jealousy and envy are present, other behaviors begin to come out. Paul also writes,

> They have become filled with every kind of wickedness, evil, greed and depravity. They are full of envy, murder, strife, deceit and malice. They are gossips, slanderers, God-haters, insolent, arrogant and boastful; they invent ways of doing evil; they disobey their parents; they are senseless, faithless, heartless, ruthless.
>
> Romans 1:29-31

The only people who desire relationships with people like this are people who are like this. Our envy causes us to become angry and bitter people who begin acting in malicious ways toward others. We push people away from us through our behavior. It alienates us from those around us.

What are the indicators that jealousy is taking control?

- We can never be positive about others. We're always negative.
- We become self-promoting, always talking about ourselves.

If you find that your friends are abandoning you, it might be time to open your book and take a look inside. In other words, take a look at yourself and see if your jealousy is the cause.

Sickness

The Bible says, "A heart at peace gives life to the body, but envy rots the bones" (Proverbs 14:30). Our envy and jealousy cause us physical problems. Here's why. Negative, self-centered people who are jealous have more stress in their life, and stress causes physical problems. A progression occurs. This is illustrated below.

The Progression of Sickness

Lack Joy

⇩

Discouragement

⇩

Stress

⇩

Sickness

- **We lack joy.** We live for the wrong purposes and our expectations are not met.
- **The absence of joy leads to discouragement.** We become discouraged and emotionally respond with negative behaviors.

- **The presence of discouragement leads to stress.** We begin to self-destruct and affect others in a negative way.
- **The presence of stress leads to sickness.** Our stress causes the body to lose balance and become unhealthy.

Violence

Paul deals with this issue. He writes, "They are full of envy, murder, strife, deceit and malice" (Romans 1:29). Envy is connected with violent and aggressive behavior. James states, "You want something but don't get it. You kill and covet, but you cannot have what you want" (James 4:2). Did you hear the story about Lisa Nowak, the female astronaut who traveled from Texas to Florida to physically and violently confront the girlfriend of her ex-boyfriend, William Oefelein, another astronaut? You mean people in NASA have problems, too? You better believe it! I'm thinking she was a little jealous, what about you?

If you're a violent person, some possible causes of that behavior are envy and jealousy. You can't control the success of someone else, so you try to take control through physical force. There's also something called misdirected violence. You might be envious and jealous of someone at work, which turns into anger, but you can't take it out on your boss. What do you do? You take it out on your wife or husband, kids, and friends who've done nothing wrong. What's the cure?

The Cure for Type "B" Jealousy

What do we do if we're victims of Type "B" jealousy? There's hope through a three-step process.

Change Your Heart

Get a new passion. Have you noticed we tend to become passionate about the things we spend time doing? Peter gives instruction to "...rid yourselves of all malice and all deceit, hypocrisy, envy, and slander of every kind. Like newborn babies, crave pure spiritual milk, so that by it you may grow up in your salvation, now that you have tasted that the Lord is good" (1 Peter 2:1-3). We're to be "cravers"! I'm thinking "chocolate" right now. Seriously. I'm specifically thinking about some Dove dark chocolate nuggets I have that I hid in my closet to keep away from my kids. Hold on a minute while I go consume one.

I'm back after about two minutes, and I had not one, but two! They were "so good"! I'm a sucker for chocolate. Wouldn't it be cool to crave God as much as we crave _____? I don't know how you would fill in the blank. We know what babies crave—milk! Believe me, I know! This is the illustration Paul gives to us. So what is our pure spiritual milk? It's not something we want that's in someone else's fridge; it's what we receive from God. It's His Word, and it sustains us. The milk we need is His instruction. We need to be listening to what God says about who we are to be. The more we hear from Him, the more we desire Him. We crave Him. And guess what? He's better than chocolate!

Stay Busy Helping Others

We are to serve one another in love. Paul writes, "You, my brothers, were called to be free. But do not use your freedom to indulge the sinful nature; rather, serve one another in love" (Galatians 5:13). A sign that we're growing up spiritually is our becoming more concerned about serving than being served. We become humble and lose our pride. Our service for others changes our hearts because we know God is using us to change the world. This leads to the last cure.

Celebrate the Success of Others

Paul writes, "Rejoice with those who rejoice…" (Romans 12:15). I'm singing the lyrics of the song "Celebration" by Kool and the Gang in my mind as I write. We are to celebrate good times. The good times come when we measure up, when we become like Christ. It's not only about our becoming like Christ, it's about others becoming like Christ. We celebrate their achievements. We also celebrate when God blesses them with more influence or more possessions that can be used to advance His work. Our celebrating others is a sign of our maturity. Celebration is also a sign of our love. We are thrilled they are becoming who God created them to be. After all, that's all He asks!

Dear God,
I confess to You that I have a jealous heart. I have been listening to the people of this world tell me the standard for my life. I know this is wrong. I commit right now to listen to You and allow You to determine the standard of measurement for my life. God, please help me to live up to what You created me to be—nothing more and nothing less.

Chapter Eight

Stressed Out and Ready to Change: Overcoming Anxiousness

Do not be anxious about anything, but in everything, by prayer and petition, with thanksgiving, present your requests to God.

Philippians 4:6

Cast all your anxiety on him because he cares for you.

1 Peter 5:7

Have you ever seen one of those lists that help you determine how much stress you have in your life? You know—it lists all the events that can happen and gives each a numerical value. You add them all up to see how stressed you are. I hate those tests because, even if I didn't have stress before the test, I learn that I'm supposed to, so I start getting stressed out. I might be stressing you out just by reminding you about the last time you took one of those tests. Sorry!

Can you think of an anxious moment in your past? One of the most stressful times in my life came several years ago as I was contemplating what God wanted me to do in my professional career. To understand the situation, I need to explain the events that led up to this time.

I grew up in the home of a pastor, and because of this, my childhood centered around the church. It was all I knew. Early on, I was like most kids who dreamed about being a fireman or a policeman. That dream changed as I entered high school. We lived in Pensacola, a navy town. The base there is used to train pilots, and I had the opportunity to get to know some of them as they became members of our church. I could see myself in the cockpit of a fighter jet flying through the sky. That sounded really cool. One problem—I didn't like the sensation of losing my stomach. This, I feared, would be a major obstacle.

As I continued to progress through school, I had some really significant spiritual experiences. One, in particular, stands out in my mind. We were attending a retreat at a location out of town. God used the guest speaker, who was there to challenge us, to impact my life in an amazing way. I had drifted away from my faith, and God used that time to show me the error of my ways. The experience led me to commit myself to be used by God in a new and fresh way.

A couple of years passed and I found myself at the national meeting of our church's denomination, which was being held in Houston, Texas. It was a tradition for our family to take vacation time and travel to this event. The big moment during the convention came when Billy Graham spoke at the Houston Astrodome. He challenged us about ministry involvement, and we witnessed hundreds of missionaries being commissioned to work on the mission field. It was awesome! I was moved by what I heard and saw and made a decision to commit my life to serve God in full-time ministry.

After graduating from high school, I attended Samford University in Birmingham, Alabama. Samford was a private Christian school with a great academic reputation. The school was very generous toward students whose parents were in the ministry by giving a large discount toward tuition. Because of this, many preacher's kids attended. I began to notice something about them. Several were not going into the ministry. They were majoring in other areas. This caused me to begin questioning my previous decision. Had I committed to full-time Christian service because it was familiar to me or had I really been called? I decided I had made a mistake. The result was my changing my major two times over four years and finishing school with a degree in psychology and a business minor. What to do now?

It was during college that Jennifer and I became a really hot item. We decided to get married after I graduated from school—that was, if I found a job to support us. I did! I had been an intern at Gulf Power Company in Pensacola during my college days and had really enjoyed my time there. I was fortunate to be hired by them full-time after graduation as a marketing representative, working out of the corporate office. We got married, bought a condo, let my brother-in-law move in with us (that's a different story—but a positive one), and bought a basset hound that we named Hush. Things seem to be lining up really well for me.

Jennifer still had two years of education to complete, and because we moved to Pensacola, she finished her degree in elementary education at the University of West Florida. Things seemed to be going well during the two years at Gulf Power. I didn't think much about doing anything else. There were days of frustration, which most of us experience, but it was a good job. It was also important for me to stay there because of our need for financial resources to pay for Jennifer's school. After she graduated and took her first teaching job, things changed. I started looking at my life and began to wonder if this was all there was. Would I be dealing with electricity for the rest of my life? Not that working for a power company was bad, but I began to realize it wasn't fulfilling my need for purpose in life. I began thinking about the decision I had made years earlier concerning the ministry. What should I do next?

I decided, with Jennifer's approval, to take a part-time position at a church on the west side of town as a minister of music and youth. I saw this as an opportunity to discover if this was what I should do with my life. Things went well, but I began to be stressed out. My Gulf Power job was putting a lot of pressure on me and I realized I couldn't keep up with the pace of my life. I knew I had to quit a job, so I quit working at the church. God used this in a strong way. After a few weeks I realized how much I missed what I was doing and that God really might have called me into the ministry. I needed help to process what was going on in my mind and heart.

After quitting the part-time church job, we began attending another church and getting involved in their ministries. Jennifer and I began to have a good relationship with the pastor, and he invited us out to a classy restaurant (Burger King) after church one Sunday night. I began talking with him about what was going in my life and asked him for advice. He told me something I've never forgotten. He said, "Tim, if you see the need, have the passion to meet the need, and know God has given you the ability to meet the need, that constitutes a call." Wow! The light when on! It confirmed what I was feeling. More decisions would now need to be made.

I didn't want to go back to school. I enjoyed my college experience, not because of the classes, but because of the social scene. School took a back seat to having fun. I did manage to graduate with decent grades, but I had no desire to ever attend school again. Why do I mention this? Many who work in churches vocationally have completed seminary education and received a master's degree in their specific concentration of ministry. This was especially true of ministers who worked in larger churches and who could afford to pay their staff a decent wage. But I was different; at least that's what I thought. Let the job hunt begin!

I sent out résumés to those churches I knew were looking for a student minister only to become very disappointed at the results. Not only did I not get those positions, but they also wouldn't even talk to me. The result? A stressed out Tim! I didn't like where things were headed because God didn't do what I wanted Him to do. Not receiving what you think you should receive can be a big-time stress builder. I became anxious about my next step. I could do one of two things: I could stop moving toward what I believed God was telling me to do and play golf on the course behind our house, or I could try the school thing. I tried the school thing!

I was running out of time to be accepted into seminary, with only two weeks remaining until the deadline. I managed to turn in everything that was required, and I made it in. We needed an income to support us while we were there, which meant that Jennifer needed a job in the public school system. The process normally required two separate interviews at two different times. She was hired on the spot. Finally, we needed a place to stay, and there was only one dormitory on campus in which we could afford to live. We got the last one. I think God wanted us to go, what about you? Although I was stressed about going to school, the stress began going away because I knew God's plan was better than my own. Our stress goes away when we begin to trust in God.

What really stresses you out? What do you worry about? The answers to these questions are often the cause of our anxiousness. How do you handle the worries of life? The "emotionally smart" learn how to handle pressure. Believers need to get a grip on this because of the influence we have on those who notice how we live. The "emotionally smart" use their emotions to reveal God. People should be able to determine that God is reliable through observing our emotional behavior. After all, if God is in control and has the power we claim, shouldn't we be worry-free? Many Christians find themselves in the mire of despair and heartache because of their worries. Anxiousness consumes them and they become ineffective in their service for God.

The word *anxiousness* comes from the word *anxiety*, which is the state of being uneasy or worried about what might happen.[31] The word *worry* comes from an old English word that means "to strangle, or choke."[32] Those who worry really do feel like they're being strangled or choked. Anxiousness suffocates us. It sucks the life right out of us. We allow fear to rule us, and it has a negative effect.

Author Douglas Rumford, in his book *Scared to Life*, wrote that sixty percent of our fears are totally unfounded; twenty percent are already behind us; ten percent are so petty they don't make any difference; and four to five percent of the remaining ten percent are real, but we can't do anything about them. Only five percent are real fears we can do something about.[33] Although only five percent of our fears are real, if we allow all of our fears to consume us, they make a mess of our lives.

The question is how do we live a life free from anxiousness? We need solutions so we can overcome our times of stress. There are different levels of anxiety that require different treatments. Just as depression should be treated medically because of chemical imbalances that happen in the body, the same is also true of those who suffer from severe anxiousness stemming from medical issues. Those who suffer from this type of anxiousness can't control their emotions through sheer willpower. It's a sickness that needs medical attention. I'm living proof of this!

There's another type of treatment for those who suffer anxiety from a different cause. We've learned our beliefs play a major role in our emotional responses. The same is true in regards to struggles with anxiousness. It's "belief-changing" time again. To relieve our anxiety, we must learn to change our beliefs. Unhealthy thoughts need to be replaced. False beliefs should give way to the truth. Before we discover the truth from God's Word, it's important we learn some basic information about anxiety.

The Traits of Anxiousness

There are certain traits that accompany our anxiety. These traits are associated with the five parts of life that define us. Take a look at the descriptions of each:

Emotionally

- Fear that turns into worry
- Emotional insensitivity
- Sadness
- Anger
- Overreaction
- Short-temperedness
- Obsessions
- Phobias

Mentally

- Plagued by guilt
- Extremely analytical
- Perfectionism
- An inability to make decisions

Socially

- Overly concerned about the opinions of others
- Controlling of relationship because of high expectations
- Paranoia

Physically

- Creasing of the forehead
- Sleeplessness
- Headaches
- Neck aches
- High blood pressure
- Looking older
- Heart disease
- Asthma
- Kidney malfunctions
- Skin disorders
- Frequent infections[34]

Spiritually

- We play the role of God by taking control
- Disobedience

The Causes of Anxiousness

There are two causes that play a significant role in our becoming anxious.

Cause #1 – We Have Unrealistic Expectations About the Future

We become depressed because people or situations don't meet our unrealistic expectations. This happens in the present. Anxiousness happens when we imagine our expectations are not met in the future. Do you remember the definition for the word *anxiety*? Anxiety is the state of being uneasy or "worried about what might happen." It hasn't happened yet. The important word in that definition is *may*. We often become worried and anxious about something that has a very small likelihood of happening in the future, yet the possibility of this event overwhelms us. We can't seem to move past our feelings over what might come.

Cause #2 – Fear

The primary emotion driving our anxiousness is fear. Daniel Goleman wrote about our anxiety. He states that our brain "fixates attention on the threat at hand, forcing the mind to obsess about how to handle it and ignore anything else for the time being. Worry is, in a sense, a rehearsal of what might go wrong and how to deal with it; the task of worrying is to come up with positive solutions for life's perils by anticipating dangers before they arise. The difficulty is with chronic, repetitive worries, the kind that recycle on and on and never get any nearer a positive solution."[35] He's right on!

There are many who don't find positive solutions because they're not focused on solutions, they're focused on the possibility of the event itself. They can't think realistically about the future because their vision of the future is distorted. Past events may be the culprit. They believe that because something happened in the past, it will happen in the future. Because of this, they anticipate hurt. They fear the potential of that hurt. They expect the worst and can't accept that there might be an alternate outcome. Although they fixate on the hurt that is to come, they do nothing to keep it from occurring. Their attention is on future pain, not in how to avoid it. They become frozen in their fear. Guess what? Big surprise! It leads to other problems. This fear grows into emotional disorders.

The Disorders Caused by Anxiousness

Anxiousness can affect us in many ways and it shows itself in many different forms. There are several anxiety disorders. They include the following:

- **Generalized Anxiety Disorder** – We worry excessively over events that aren't likely to occur.[36]
- **Social Anxiety Disorder** – We avoid people because of our concern about our behavior when in the presence of others.[37]
- **Obsessive Compulsive Disorder** (OCD) – We are obsessed with a certain belief and feel we must perform some behavior to relieve ourselves of the obsession.[38] For example, the fear of germs leads to the continual washing of hands. Fear of someone peeking in your room at night leads to opening and shutting the blinds over and over again. (Personal flashback!). The fear of not being forgiven of sins leads to praying for the forgiveness of those sins over and over again. (Me, again!).
- **Post-traumatic Stress Disorder** – We are overwhelmed by a past tragedy and can't move past the event.[39] We may imagine that something similar will happen again in our future. We may become stuck in our fear. People who have experienced car accidents are highly prone to this.
- **Panic Disorder** – We are suddenly overcome by intense fear.[40] We feel out of control and we panic.

I mentioned that I have suffered from depression in my childhood and in my adult life. My depression has occurred because of an unrealistic expectation that everyone should like me. My fear in those depressed moments was that people wouldn't like me. I worried about the future or the outcome

of certain decisions because of this. That worry was anxiousness, which grew into a disorder.

I wrote about my personal struggles at the beginning
of this book and mentioned that I suffer from OCD. Some
examples were given above of repetitive behaviors. Although
I'm not consumed with germs on my hands, I do have an
unusual fear about my toothbrush touching my wife's. I also
had a fear that God would not forgive me of my sins unless
I asked for forgiveness in a certain way, not stumbling over
my words. This led me to pray the same prayer over and
over again until I said it just right. It also affected the time I
spent in Bible study. I would find myself reading the same
Scripture over and over again because of the fear I had read
a word in the wrong way, thinking God would be displeased
with me.

Did you ever see the movie, *Groundhog Day,* with Bill
Murray? It's one of my favorites. Murray plays the main character who is an obnoxious weather man, a womanizer, and
your basic lowlife. He takes advantage of people and does
whatever he can to keep inflating his already big ego. It's
Groundhog Day and he's reporting on the big rat-like animal
(no offense to those who might live in Punxsutawney) that
comes out of his hole to see if he sees his shadow. Actually,
the rat-like animal (groundhog) is pretty cool!

The TV crew gets snowed in and can't go back to the big
city, so they have to stay in town one more night. He wakes
up the next morning and it's Groundhog Day all over again.
Of course, this really freaks him out. Anyway, he keeps
reliving this day over and over again until his heart changes
and he becomes a caring man. He falls in love and—you got
it—finally wakes up the day after Groundhog Day.

You're probably wondering how I'm going to make a
connection with this movie and my life. Here it is. When I
was living in the worst moments of my obsessive compul-
siveness, I felt like it was Groundhog Day. It was like I was

stuck and I kept replaying the same thing over and over and over again, and I couldn't move on. That is, until I fell in love. Not with a woman, but with God. I've known God a long time. He and I've been connected since I was a kid, but somewhere along the way I started trusting in myself more than Him. That self-love thing! No wonder I was anxious. Trusting in self should bring fear. When my love for Him began to grow again, I began to trust Him more and more, and my fear began to go away. I moved past my Groundhog Day. God began to heal my heart and mind. How can we be healed?

The Healing Process for Anxiousness

Two important passages of Scripture provide instruction for us as we look to God for healing. Paul writes about how we are to respond emotionally in a letter to the church at Philippi:

Rejoice in the Lord always. I will say it again: Rejoice! Let your gentleness be evident to all. The Lord is near. Do not be anxious about anything, but in everything, by prayer and petition, with thanks-giving, present your requests to God. And the peace of God, which transcends all understanding, will guard your hearts and your minds in Christ Jesus.
Philippians 4:4-7

A second passage is also "huge" (in other words—really important)! Peter writes the following:

Humble yourselves, therefore, under God's mighty hand, that he may lift you up in due time. Cast all your anxiety on him because he cares for you. Be self-controlled and alert. Your enemy the devil prowls around like a roaring lion looking for someone to devour. Resist him, standing firm in the faith, because you know that your brothers throughout the world are undergoing the same kind of sufferings. And the God of all grace, who called you to his eternal glory in Christ, after you have suffered a little while, will himself restore you and make you strong, firm and steadfast. To him be the power for ever and ever. Amen.

1 Peter 5:6-11

The Scriptures indicate what we can do to overcome anxiousness. They include:

Be Environmentally Aware

We are to be alert (1 Peter 5:8). This means we are to know what's going on around us. Jesus says, "Be careful, or your hearts will be weighed down with dissipation, drunkenness and the anxieties of life, and that day will close on you unexpectedly like a trap" (Luke 21:34). He knows we need to be careful about how we relate to our circumstances. He also knows the ease by which we can find ourselves trapped in an unhealthy emotional state. Listen again to Peter's words: "Be self-controlled and alert. Your enemy the devil prowls around like a roaring lion looking for someone to devour" (1 Peter 5:8). There are two important truths for us to think about:

- **Satan wants me to be weak and to fail**. He wants to keep me down. Solomon writes, "An anxious heart weighs a man down..." (Proverbs 12:25). How true this is. Jesus acknowledges the work of evil when He says, "The thief comes only to steal and kill and destroy; I have come that they may have life, and have it to the full" (John 10:10). Satan wants to steal our minds and hearts. What does God want?

- **God wants me to be strong and to succeed.** The strong manage life well. We learn from Peter's words that God wants to restore us and make us "strong, firm and steadfast" (1 Peter 5:10). Suffering from anxiousness isn't God's plan for your life. It's also not God's plan for my life. God wants us to overcome it. He wants to help us. Jesus says, "Come to me, all you who are weary and burdened, and I will give you rest" (Matthew 11:28). What an awesome promise! He wants to help us through the emotional low points of life. We must trust in Him to experience help. There's no need to be anxious about anything when He's in control.

Be Self-Aware

This also relates to our being alert (1 Peter 5:8). We need to be aware of our feelings that lead to emotional difficulty. There are some important questions to ask ourselves:

- **Am I afraid?** Remember, fear causes me to worry. Paul writes to Timothy, "For God hath not given us the spirit of fear; but of power, and of love, and of a sound mind" (2 Timothy 1:7). When we become fearful, we lose power, we are no longer loving, and we no longer make sound decisions. It clouds our thinking. Jesus speaks powerful words when He calms the waters during a severe storm. He says to His disciples, "Why are you so afraid? Do you still have no faith?" (Mark 4:40). The words of Jesus point out something about our worry and fear. Our fear comes from a lack of faith. We know we have a trust problem when there is fear. It begins to rule us when we trust in someone or something other than God.

We often redirect our trust and place it in what we feel will bring us happiness. This happiness is short-lived and doesn't last. Everything we trust in other than God is temporary in nature. We fear that what we trust in will end in the future because it *will* end in the future! God is eternal, and trusting in Him brings eternal joy.

- **Am I worried?** There is a difference between concern and worry. Jesus clearly tells us not to worry. He says, "Therefore I tell you, do not worry about your life, what you will eat or drink; or about your body, what you will wear. Is not life more important than food, and the body more important than clothes? ...O you of little faith? So do not worry, saying, 'What shall we eat?' or 'What shall we drink?' or 'What shall we wear?' For the pagans run after all these things, and your heavenly Father knows that you need them. [33]But seek first his kingdom and his righteousness, and all these things will be given to you as well. Therefore do not worry about tomorrow, for tomorrow will worry about itself. Each day has enough trouble of its own" (Matthew 6:25, 30-34).

We need to understand the difference between concern and worry. Stoop addresses this. He writes, "Concern focuses on controllable behavior and events; worry focuses on events and behavior that are beyond our control. Worry is really an attempt to control the future. ...Worry is our godlike push into the future, attempting to shape it the way we want."[41] There's a close connection between this statement and the next question.

- **Do I attempt to control the outcome of situations?**
  If I do, I've taken control and I'm now playing God.
  I should worry because I can't realistically control
  all aspects of my life. There's reason to be anxious.

Be Self-Controlled

We need to do something to stop our behavior by practicing self-control and making some wise decisions. There
really is a psychological theory called "Stop Therapy."
I learned about it in college. We say to ourselves, "Stop."
When we hear the word *stop*, we are programmed to stop
because danger is on the horizon. We've been taught this
since childhood. I've also heard of people using a loose
rubber band around their wrist. They pop it against their
skin when they catch themselves worrying. They do this in
places where they can't say out loud the word *stop*. This gets
their attention and they choose to redirect their thoughts.
This stops their worrying and encourages them to start doing
something else. Actually, we are to start doing two things.
This is awesome!

Peter writes,

> Humble yourselves, therefore, under God's mighty
> hand, that he may lift you up in due time. Cast all
> your anxiety on him because he cares for you. Be
> self-controlled and alert. Your enemy the devil prowls
> around like a roaring lion looking for someone to
> devour.
> 1 Peter 5:6-8

How about a learning exercise? Circle the words *humble*
and *cast* in the Scripture above. Both are actions we control.
We choose to place ourselves under God's control, an act of
humility, because we realize we're incapable of controlling

all things. We choose to cast our anxiety on God, knowing He cares for us. We stop worrying because we know we don't have to worry about our needs being met. God cares for us and will meet our needs. He is faithful. This is really, really cool. Read this next statement out loud, that is, if you are in a place where people won't think you're crazy. What am I talking about? Who cares what they think, right? Are you ready to read it out loud? I know what you're probably thinking—*All right, then, what am I supposed to say?* Okay! Here it is. Say it out loud: "It's not our job to meet our needs; it's God's job!" Wasn't that fun? Is it a little liberating? Let's do it again. Say it out loud one more time: "It's not our job to meet our needs; it's God's job!" We become anxious and stressed when we take control and trust in our own ability to meet our needs. We try to do something by ourselves that isn't intended for us to do alone. So what is our job? Our job is to obey Him. That's all we have to be concerned about. Did you catch the word *concern*? We don't have to worry about obedience; we have to be concerned about it. We should make it a priority, knowing the effect it can have on us if we don't.

Back to God's command! We are commanded to cast our anxiety on Him. But how? The answer is through prayer. Paul writes to the church at Philippi, "Do not be anxious about anything, but in everything, by prayer and petition, with thanksgiving, present your requests to God. And the peace of God, which transcends all understanding, will guard your hearts and your minds in Christ Jesus" (Philippians 4:6-7). Prayer brings peace. Since we've started saying things out loud, why don't you say what we just read: "Prayer brings peace." Relief of anxiety requires our faithful prayer. Here's why it works: Praying to God redirects our attention to God. Prayer is the tool used to change us. We are to do the following:

- **Submit yourself to God**. James writes, "But he gives us more grace. That is why Scripture says: 'God opposes the proud but gives grace to the humble.' Submit yourselves, then, to God. Resist the devil, and he will flee from you" (James 4:6-7). Remember, God didn't give us the spirit of fear; therefore, it must come from the opposing force. It comes from Satan. If I have fear, I've submitted to the wrong power.

I submit my life to God when I give Him control of everything. I lose my pride and willingly allow Him to be the One who meets my needs. I need to pray about this. My prayer is a prayer of confession. I confess to God that I've not submitted to Him and I claim His forgiveness. Do you remember what the Bible says about confession? The Scripture teaches, "If we confess our sins, he is faithful and just and will forgive us our sins and purify us from all unrighteousness" (1 John 1:9). Once again, we learned about this earlier in the book. We learned that confession is the evidence we have repented, we have turned toward God. We do this through prayer. Our prayer of confession turns our face toward Him.

Confession to God and to others about our failures is an indication we are truly submitting to Him. It helps bring healing. This was true in my life. My healing began when I confessed my obsessive compulsive behavior to Jennifer, my wife. It was the turning point for me. I had confessed my failures many times to God, but I had reverted right back to those same behaviors. I had turned toward God, but I didn't move in the right direction. Just facing God isn't enough. My life radically changed when I confessed to Jennifer. It was actual movement in the right direction. I had done something. I had proven by my action that I had repented and my heart had changed. Talk about a good day! That was a really good day!

- **Trust God for everything**. Once again, remember Paul's words: "Do not be anxious about anything, but in everything, by prayer and petition, with thanksgiving, present your requests to God" (Philippians 4:6). I'm into circling words all of a sudden. If you have a pen or pencil with you, circle the phrase "but in everything." We have to trust Him with everything. The indicator we are not trusting God with everything is our worry. That was a really big statement. I hope you got it! The presence of worry confirms our need to pray about the area of life we have taken back. What is it? We should make up our minds not to worry about anything. This decision should occur before we face challenges.

  Jesus says, "But make up your mind not to worry beforehand how you will defend yourselves. For I will give you words and wisdom that none of your adversaries will be able to resist or contradict" (Luke 21:14-15). They could worry about what they were going to say or they could trust in God. Trusting in God would require them to allow Him to control what they would say. When we change our trust, anxiousness goes away.

  Do you remember how to do this? It's still through prayer! This is a prayer of faith. We state our trust in God and that our faith is in Him. This reminds us where our faith should be. It's also a commitment to action. We commit to trust in Him and not ourselves. We ask Him to be the "Lord" and ruler of every part of us, including our thought life.

- **Be Thankful**. Listen again to the instruction: "Do not be anxious about anything, but in everything, by prayer and petition, with thanksgiving, present your requests to God" (Philippians 4:6). We are to do everything with thanksgiving in our hearts. How do we show our thankfulness? Through prayer! Prayer really must be important! This is a different prayer. We have prayed a prayer of confession and a prayer of faith; now we're to pray a prayer of thanksgiving. We should be thanking God that we have no reason to worry because our faith is in Him. We should thank Him for being in control of our lives. We should also thank Him for His presence, His direction, and His strength.

Be Under Control

The Bible states,
And the God of all grace, who called you to his eternal glory in Christ, after you have suffered a little while, will himself restore you and make you strong, firm and steadfast. To him be the power for ever and ever. Amen.

1 Peter 5:10-11

God restores us. The restoration process is now complete. We are no longer in control; we are under control. When we follow the healing process, we are under God's control. What does that mean? The Bible just told us what happens to us. Circle the words *strong*, *firm*, and *steadfast* in the Scripture from above.

- **We are strong because we are not afraid**. This sounds emotionally healthy to me. We are strong when we trust in God. We are weak when we trust in ourselves. Worry is a sign of spiritual weakness. Those who are strong aren't overcome because they have proper thoughts about their circumstances. There's no need to worry—God is in control! The Psalmist writes, "The LORD is my light and my salvation—whom shall I fear? The LORD is the stronghold of my life—of whom shall I be afraid?" (Psalm 27:1).

- **We stand firm because we have faith**. This sounds emotionally healthy to me. We don't compromise our faith in God. We no longer do everything in fear; we now do everything in love. Paul writes, "Be on your guard; stand firm in the faith; be men of courage; be strong. Do everything in love" (1 Corinthians 16:13-14). We serve ourselves when we place faith in ourselves. This is a life absent of outward love. It's only directed inward. We serve others because of our faith in God. That means if we have a service problem, we have a faith problem. Our love is to be directed outward, positively affecting those around us.

- **We are steadfast because we are prepared**. This sounds emotionally healthy to me. We are consistent in our responses. Why? Because we have prepared ourselves not to worry by being environmentally aware, self-aware, self-controlled, and under control. We've followed the steps to overcoming anxiousness.

Are you stressed out? That's not God's plan for your life. Are you worried about life? That's also not God's plan for you. It's a sign you're not letting God be in control. Stop! Stop it by starting something new. Redirect your mind and heart back to God. Do it right now through prayer.

God,

I cast my anxiety on You. I confess to You that I have been trusting in myself and have not submitted to You. I know I have been wrong. I commit myself to trust in You and You alone. Thank You for loving me and meeting my needs. I thank You that I have nothing to fear, for You are with me!

Chapter Nine

The Battle of the Grudge: Overcoming Bitterness

Get rid of all bitterness, rage and anger, brawling and
slander, along with every form of malice. Be kind
and compassionate to one another, forgiving each
other, just as in Christ God forgave you.

Ephesians 4:31-32

Most of us have become bitter about something over the
course of our lives. Think about some of your actions
and emotions. Our anger, rage, fighting, verbal abuse, or
talking poorly about other people can be a sign we have a
bitterness problem.

Pastor Paul Yonggi Cho knows what it means to struggle
with bitterness. Cho is the pastor of the largest church in
the world. Several years ago, his ministry was beginning to
expand internationally and he was faced with these bitter
feelings. Mark Buchanan, in his book *Your God is Too Safe*,
details his struggle. He writes,

He told God, "I will go anywhere to preach the gospel
except Japan." He hated the Japanese with gut-deep
loathing because of what Japanese troops had done

to the Korean people and to members of Yonggi Cho's own family during WWII. The Japanese were his Ninevites. Through a combination of a prolonged inner struggle, several direct challenges from others, and finally an urgent and starkly worded invitation, Cho felt called by God to preach in Japan. He went, but he went with bitterness. His first speaking engagement was to a pastor's conference of 1,000 Japanese pastors. Cho stood up to speak, and what came out of his mouth was this: "I hate you. I hate you. I hate you." And then he broke and wept. He was both brimming and desolate with hatred. At first one, then two, then all 1,000 pastors stood up. One by one they walked up to Yonggi Cho, knelt at his feet and asked forgiveness for what they and their people had done to him and his people. As this went on, God changed Yonggi Cho. The Lord put a single message in his heart and mouth: "I love you. I love you. I love you."[42]

Are you bitter? Have you been holding on to events that have occurred in your past? Do you begrudge people because of this? Pastor Cho found the freedom that all who struggle with bitterness need to find. He was able to direct his attention away from hurtful events and toward hurting people. Bitter people struggle through life and have a hard time making sense of events that have occurred in their past. Unfortunately, they've allowed their circumstances to control them. Here's some good news! It's possible for them to move past their circumstances and find peace.

How about another example? Three people were shot to death on June 17, 1966, in the Lafayette Grill in Paterson, New Jersey. A black boxer named Rubin "Hurricane" Carter and an acquaintance were charged and convicted of the crime although they were innocent. Rubin maintained his claim that he did nothing wrong and was eventually released after serving nineteen years in prison. He shared his feelings toward the injustice he experienced in his life.

> The question invariably arises, it has before and it will again: "Rubin, are you bitter?" And in answer to that I will say, "After all that's been said and done—the fact that the most productive years of my life, between the ages of twenty-nine and fifty, have been stolen; the fact that I was deprived of seeing my children grow up—wouldn't you think I would have a right to be bitter? Wouldn't anyone under those circumstances have a right to be bitter? In fact, it would be very easy to be bitter. But that has never been my nature, or my lot, to do things the easy way. If I have learned nothing else in my life, I've learned that bitterness only consumes the vessel that contains it. And for me to permit bitterness to control or to infect my life in any way whatsoever would be to allow those who imprisoned me to take even more than the 22 years they've already taken. Now that would make me an accomplice to their crime."[43]

Have you become an accomplice to the crime that others have committed against you? If you do, you lose hope. If you do, you lose the joy of life. A false belief is held that circumstances are the determining factor of your happiness. The truth is your circumstances don't make you happy or unhappy; rather, what you believe about your circumstances makes the difference. If you buy into this false belief, you become bitter and resentful.

Max Lucado writes,

> Resentment is when you let your hurt become hate.
> Resentment is when you allow what is eating you to

eat you up. Resentment is when you poke, stoke, feed, and fan the fire, stirring the flames and reliving the pain. Resentment is the deliberate decision to nurse the offense until it becomes a black, furry, growling grudge.[44]

I don't know about you, but I don't want to be resentful. The bitter tend to blame others for their condition and refuse to forgive them. This leads to the holding of grudges. People who struggle with bitterness don't see they're harming themselves. They're causing themselves stress that results in a physical and emotional breakdown. An unforgiving spirit brings resentment and leads to aggressive behavior. They begin experiencing animosity toward other people. They think unhealthy thoughts and begin imagining ways to inflict pain. They believe their bitterness is not their fault; it's the fault of the one who has harmed them.

I know this is true because I've been a "grudger." It is really easy for me to begin having these feelings. Every time I do, without fail, it's because I feel sorry for myself. Poor, pitiful me! I can't believe someone would treat me badly and I would want them to pay. Why? Because I'm mad! Let the pouting begin. Don't I sound like a lovely person to hang out with? I'm learning to become compassionate. God cares for me not because of what I do, but because of who I am. This is compassion. I'm beginning to do the same thing. I'm learning to care for people, not because of what they do, but because of who they are. Believe me, this makes life much better.

It's Not My Problem!

People have the "It's Not My Problem" attitude when they become bitter. They don't feel like they're the cause of the mess they're in (better known as their bitterness). They think someone else is at fault and should be the one to clean it up. This is a false belief. Once again, here's some truth: No one makes us bitter; we choose if for ourselves.

The apostle Paul has something to say about bitterness in the letter to the church at Ephesus. He writes,

> Do not let any unwholesome talk come out of your mouths, but only what is helpful for building others up according to their needs, that it may benefit those who listen. And do not grieve the Holy Spirit of God, with whom you were sealed for the day of redemption. Get rid of all bitterness, rage and anger, brawling and slander, along with every form of malice. Be kind and compassionate to one another, forgiving each other, just as in Christ God forgave you.
>
> Ephesians 4:29-32

We're instructed to get rid of all bitterness. Why? It's the beginning of aggressive behavior that's aimed at harming, not helping, other people. Don Colbert, a physician and expert in the area of emotional health, writes that "over time, resentment and bitterness grow stronger and stronger. These aren't emotions that diminish over time."[45] How true this is! The stronger they grow, the angrier we become and the more we long to lash out at others. This grieves the Holy Spirit. I sound like a broken record, but remember, everything the Holy Spirit leads us to do is for the purpose of building others up, not destroying them. It's time for some basic information about bitterness.

The Indicators of Bitterness

How can I know if I'm bitter? One way I can know is if the indicators tell me so (a little rhyming for ya!). So what are they? Our emotions affect every area of life. That means, if we become bitter, then bitterness affects every area of our lives. Remember, there are five areas that define us. They include our emotional, mental, social, physical, and spiritual lives. Let's take a look at how bitterness affects each.

Emotional Life – We Respond with Rage and Anger

We've learned through the passage of Scripture in Ephesians how it affects us in this area. The primary emotion that kicks in when we are bitter is anger. Our anger causes us spiritual problems. James writes, "For man's anger does not bring about the righteous life that God desires" (James 1:20). Consider two types of anger. Aggressive anger ("hot" anger) is marked by violence and screaming. Passive aggressive anger ("cold" anger) is more silent and shows itself through manipulation and control. Bitterness can display itself through both types of anger but often is shown through "cold" passive aggressive anger. Our silence becomes deafening and our manipulative actions become piercing. Does this describe you?

Mental Life – We Become Hypercritical of Other People, Complain About Them, and Concentrate Our Attention on the Past

Our mental life is defined by what we think. We can tell what we are thinking by listening to what we say. Those who are thinking in an unhealthy way tend to complain. Some complain a lot. Job writes, "I loathe my very life; therefore I will give free rein to my complaint and speak out in the bitterness of my soul" (Job 10:1). Again, we begin believing we're the way we are because of what other people have done to us in the past. We blame them for our condition. Because of this, we keep looking behind us and never in front of us. In other words, we keep thinking about what has happened to us in the past and refuse to think about the changes we need to make now that will affect our future in a positive way. We have baggage and we can't get our attention off it.

I have baggage, you have baggage, and we all have baggage. Les Parrott and Neil Clark Warren, in their book *Love the Life You Live,* write that "until you learn to move past your past, you will never be able to understand your incalculable value or experience profound significance at your very core."[46] They add that "The healthy person does not dwell excessively on the past. He understands the past, but he doesn't get stuck in it."[47] For example, the unhealthy person believes that they can't be any better than they are because they had parents who abused them or because of some other difficult event. They're stuck and can't move on in a healthy way. It's just not true! Does this describe you?

Social Life – We Curse Others, Seek Revenge, Envy, and Are Happy When Others Fail

Just in case you haven't figured this out, these attributes are not used to maintain a good and healthy relationship. We've already learned about this, but a good learning exercise is repetition, so here we go. Remember what Paul teaches us. He writes, "Do not let any unwholesome talk come out of your mouths..." (Ephesians 4:29). Our words, used in an unwholesome way, don't build people up and bring health to the relationship. When we speak out aggressively, we become destructive, not constructive. Those who speak this way seek revenge against others. This goes against God's instruction for us. We read, "Do not seek revenge or bear a grudge against one of your people...." (Leviticus 19:18). We begin finding pleasure in their failure. Sounds like the problem I mentioned earlier that pastors have when others fall. We're taught not to feel this way. The Bible says, "Do not gloat when your enemy falls; when he stumbles, do not let your heart rejoice" (Proverbs 24:17).

Envy causes bitterness and disorder. Relationships begin to break down. James writes, "For where you have envy and selfish ambition, there you find disorder...." (James 3:16). Disorder is a social problem, but it's a social problem that can be corrected.

Physical Life – We Experience Headaches, Ulcers, Sleeplessness, Heart Attacks, Anxiety, Fear, Tension, and Depression

The Scripture teaches us that "...envy rots the bones" (Proverbs 14:30). "Bone Rot" is not an exciting physical condition to experience. As we've learned, our emotional problems cause us stress, which affects our physical make-up. It's ironic that when we intend to harm others through our bitterness, we end up causing ourselves pain and suffering physically. Does this describe you?

Spiritual Life – We Begin Disobeying God

James taught, "*For where you have envy and selfish ambition, there you find disorder and every evil practice.*" (James 3:16). Envy and selfish ambition (causes of our bitterness) not only lead to disorder, they also lead us to act out in evil ways. It leads to sin. Our bitterness triggers hateful words and actions that are used purposefully for destruction. We load our "spiritual rifles" and begin firing away, shooting people down, leading them away from God. We become puppets in the devil's hands. We allow him to pull the strings. We act out to harm others when, in truth, we're hurting ourselves by putting strain on our fellowship with God.

The Causes of Bitterness

Where does our bitterness come from? Bitterness come from within, not from without. Bitterness comes from what is going on inside of us, not what is happening around us. The name for this condition is called "unforgiveness." We experience unforgiveness in three areas.

We Don't Get What We Want

Hannah, from Old Testament times, is a great example of this. She desperately wanted a son and had not received one. The Bible describes her this way: "In bitterness of soul Hannah wept much and prayed to the LORD" (1 Samuel 1:10). She hadn't received what she wanted and was bitter in soul because of this. I can relate!

A turning point in my professional life happened back in 1996. It was the year I became the pastor at Woodland. So much happened leading up to that event. It really began as I was serving in my first full-time position as a minister of music and youth in 1990. I had studied to become a student minister while in seminary and was serving in a church in Gulf Breeze, Florida. The pastor of the church was quickly coming to the end of his career and was preparing to enter retirement. By the way, retirement for him was ending his full-time pastoral career and redirecting his efforts in ministry to help pastors and churches around the state. What a great example of someone who continues to use his life as an investment.

As his retirement approached, I felt like God was dealing with me. I had grown up in the home of a pastor and was very familiar with the life of someone who led the church. Up until this time, I had no desire whatsoever to take that type of a position in a church. The big obstacle for me was not being in charge (I love that) or being in front of people

(I love that, too), it was preparing messages every week. It just seemed like a really stressful thing to do. God began to work on me in this area. During my daily quiet time, I would read the Scriptures and begin noticing things I hadn't noticed before. If you're a student of the Bible, you've probably experienced the same thing. Something unique happened to me during this time. I began to see patterns in God's Word. That probably sounds weird. I didn't see some code or secret; I simply began noticing how things connected together in the Scripture to teach spiritual principles. God was opening my eyes in a new way. I suddenly had a huge passion to share this with others. He was overcoming the anxiety I experienced connected to the study and preparation needed to speak for Him and was showing that He would be there to be the revealer. He would tell me what I needed to say.

This changed everything for me. A desire in me began to grow to become a pastor. I really believed God was possibly preparing me to become the pastor in the church I was serving. Jennifer and I had one of our most significant spiritual experiences together as we tried to figure this out. We decided to go away for a few days and pray and ask God for His direction. Things just seemed to make sense that God was leading me into this position. Another factor in all of this was something that was happening in our personal lives. Jennifer was pregnant with our first child and it was exciting to think we would be able to serve in my passion and stay where we were. After coming back from the trip, we shared what we thought God was up to with someone on the search team who was looking for our new pastor. They began praying with us and told other members on the team. They decided that this wasn't God's plan for the church. We were disappointed, but we accepted the decision and knew God had something amazing prepared for us in the future.

Shortly after this event, I received a phone call from someone I knew who was on staff at a church in Jacksonville,

Florida. They were looking for a full-time student minister. Although I had enjoyed doing the music thing, it was appealing to me to be able to pastor over a group of students. It was a really large church and I would be serving over the same number of people in a student ministry that I would have been as the pastor of my current church. Although I knew God was leading me to be a pastor, I also knew I had more to learn. I was honest with the church in Jacksonville and told them I believed God would eventually lead me into a position as pastor. They accepted this. I had a peace about the invitation and took the job.

Five years passed and God blessed the ministry. What I had hoped would happen did happen. The pastor of the church gave me additional pastoral responsibilities, even giving me opportunities to preach. I was also performing weddings and funerals and was involved in baptizing those who had become new believers. Although the ministry was very successful, I began to feel uneasy about continuing on as a student pastor. I began to pray again about God's will for my future.

Soon after, an opportunity came about for me to start a new church in an area that our state convention had designated as a place to begin a new work. This was really exciting for me, and I began walking through doors that were opening for me. Although this would require a big change in our financial condition, both Jennifer and I believed this was what God wanted us to do. Then something unexpected happened. Some pastors in the association of churches got upset about our plan. I couldn't believe it and became very discouraged. We had walked down this road, a long walk, toward beginning this new work and now there was a huge obstacle.

When facing an obstacle, it's important to figure out what it's all about. Either God was giving us a challenge to move through and build our faith so we could be more effective or He was closing the door for us to take this position. Both

Jennifer and I believed it was the latter. We didn't want to be a source of division among the other churches. The result was bitterness! I was so upset God had not given me something I wanted so badly. I was leading a class in our church during this time for my student leaders called "Experiencing God." The key concept in the training was to see where God was working and get involved. I thought that was what I was doing. My teaching took a really bad turn. I began sharing with the group that I couldn't figure out God's will for my own life. We began praying and asking God to reveal to us what He was doing. Then it happened.

Shortly after this experience, I'd say about two weeks, I had another phone call. A church in Bradenton, Florida, contacted me, and it was looking for a new pastor. It was a fairly new church and they were anxious to find a pastor who had vision to reach the community. They told me they just wanted someone to come and tell them what to do. Every pastor wants to hear something like that! There I was, a bitter man, when God had a plan for me all along. We accepted the position and ten years later I sit here writing about my story. God has done an awesome work through His people. Things really are changing in Bradenton because of the influence of the church. God used the experience to show me He was preparing me. I believe He was doing it to show me something about myself. First, that I needed to humbly follow Him. Second, that I was willing to make significant sacrifices to serve Him. If I had not gone through the experience, I would not have known to what extent I was willing to sacrifice for Him. The bitterness disappeared and I became more trusting of God.

Remember Hannah? She recognized her condition and prayed to God, knowing He was the solution to her problem. I have done the same. Many don't respond this way; instead, they blame God or other people for their situation. They become angry and stop. They stop growing in their spiritual walk and no longer learn to have greater faith in God.

We Focus on Our Problems and Hardships

The Bible says, "He has besieged me and surrounded me with bitterness and hardship" (Lamentations 3:5). We become bitter when life becomes hard and we notice others don't have the same struggles. We feel it's unfair. We begin making excuses like "they have an unfair advantage because of their friendships" or "they have an unfair advantage because they had the money to receive a better education." We blame God or other people for these situations. This response indicates a false belief that happiness comes from our purchasing power or our position of influence. If we don't attain these, our emotions are affected in a negative way. Some fall for the "poor me" victim mindset, just like I have in the past. Those who experience this dwell on the past. They have a hard time moving on and this behavior becomes toxic to their spiritual health. Instead of becoming better, they find themselves living their lives making excuses.

We Refuse to Forgive Others for Their Foolishness

The Bible says, "A foolish son brings grief to his father and bitterness to the one who bore him" (Proverbs 17:25). The mistakes of the foolish son can affect the father in a negative way. Can you relate? The father may even decide not to forgive the son for his foolish mistake. He becomes bitter. We can easily allow the mistakes of others to control us. We begin to believe our happiness is dependent upon their making the right decisions and not affecting us in a negative way. They're not only doing themselves a disservice, but they are also doing the same for the one who failed. This event is a learning experience for both of those involved.

The one who is affected becomes a better teacher of the one who failed when he or she is forgiving. This causes a relationship to be strengthened, not destroyed. My heart breaks when I hear of parents and children who haven't spoken to each other in years because of some past mistake. Bitterness drove them apart. Forgiveness is the only hope for healing.

The messages we tell ourselves and the feelings we nurture make the difference in whether or not we experience bitterness. What we choose to see and believe affects our outlook on life. Warren and Parrott taught this lesson using a statement about two men in jail. It goes like this: "Two men from their prison cell gaze up to see the stars. One saw constellations bright, the other, only bars."[48] It's amazing how differently two people can see the same world.

If you're bitter, let me ask you a question:. What did the person who influenced you to become bitter do to you? What hurtful attitude, words, or behaviors came your way? These hurtful behaviors from others influence us to feel a sense of hurt or loss. That's where bitterness comes from. We're bitter because we've been hurt or have lost something or someone important to us, such as an object, a relationship, or a position. What was it? What effect is your bitterness having on you now? It's time to change!

We've learned our emotions are dependent upon our beliefs. We'll not change until we change our thinking. Joseph is a great example. His brothers were jealous of him because of the attention he received from his father. Their solution was to sell him into slavery. Joseph had good reason to become bitter, but he didn't respond this way. He didn't allow the evil behavior of his brothers to cause him to experience emotional failure. Instead, he responded with these words: "You intended to harm me, but God intended it for good to accomplish what is now being done, the saving of many lives" (Genesis 50:20). God used this event in Joseph's life to place him in a position to rescue His people. It worked because Joseph didn't become bitter. I wonder what would have happened if bitterness would have set in? Our emotional behavior comes from what we say to ourselves about people and circumstances. He refused to hate his brothers. He chose to love them. We also have a choice to make. To be healed, we must let go of hate and latch on to love. If we don't, we're in for trouble. We're making ourselves miserable.

The Results of Refusing to Let Go

What happens to us when we refuse to let go? To answer this question, I want to tell you a fictional story that represents many real life situations. There once lived a thirteen-year-old boy who wanted the attention of his father. We'll call him Tony. His dad was a big-time business man and traveled all over the country, leaving his family for days on end. One day, Tony's dad promised to take him fishing on his birthday. He even bought him a new rod and reel for the big day. Well, Tony's dad loved making money more than his family, so when an opportunity came for him to make a "boatload" of cash, he was on the plane and gone again. He missed Tony's birthday. He tried to justify this by telling himself he was doing something good for his family. After all, more money meant more stuff for them.

Tony's dad had left the rod and reel for him, and his mother had the job of delivering the gift to him in his room. When Tony took it in his hands, he immediately "bummed out," knowing he had been given something he wasn't even going to be able to use. He felt like his dad didn't love him. Tony became very bitter and wanted to make his dad pay. He became very rebellious and disrespectful to him, causing his father to become stricter by laying down some firm rules, hoping this would bring his child under control. This strategy didn't work. It backfired. Tony would deliberately disobey his father, even if it meant being grounded to his room.

Tony was hurt because he felt unloved, but he still longed for a relationship. Because he didn't find it with his dad, he looked to people his own age to fill the void. He found kids who could relate to him and who also felt about their parents the way he felt about his father. They were all bitter about the love they were missing. Those in the group became the best of friends. However, this didn't take their bitterness away. In fact, they wanted to get back at their families so much that they became violent and destructive. They did this to get the attention of their parents, even if it meant bringing physical harm to others or to themselves.

You might read this story and say the boy's behavior was caused by his father's choice. Granted, things could have been much different if his father had treated the boy differently. There's no excuse for the father's behavior. He obviously had his priorities in the wrong order. But the boy had other choices available to him. No one forced Tony to become bitter. There are stories of children who have experienced terrible childhoods who never amount to anything. But there are other stories of children who have similar experiences who overcame the odds and became successful. The difference is in how they chose to respond. They didn't get stuck in their hurt. If we don't get out of our hurt, it leads to other problems in life. That's exactly what happened to Tony. He was hurt, he rebelled, he formed unhealthy relationships, and he became destructive because of his anger. This is the progression we follow when we don't move on. This is illustrated below. If you're bitter, where are you in this process?

The Progression
of Bitterness

Hurt

⇩

Rebellion

⇩

Unhealthy
Relationships

⇩

Destruction/
Death

Let's get into each part of the bitterness progression and learn more.

Hurt

Tony was hurt. He was the recipient of some self-centered behavior. That does hurt! Being hurt causes us grief, which can be crippling. To succeed emotionally, we must let go of our grief. If we don't move past our hurt, we don't make it through the grieving process and let it go. When we experience loss—whether it's from the death of a loved one, the loss of a job, the loss of a marriage partner through divorce, the loss of a close friendship, or the loss of love we have received from someone close to us (like a father)—we go through a grieving process. We move from one stage to the next. The stages include:

- **Denial** – We don't really believe it's happened to us. It doesn't seem real. We keep waiting to wake up from the nightmare.
- **Shock** – We know it's real and it paralyzes us. We can't function in a normal way.
- **Guilt** – We begin feeling it's somehow our fault.
- **Depression** – We know we can't change what has happened and we become discouraged.
- **Anger** – We begin blaming the other person and act out aggressively to make them experience pain.
- **Bargaining** – We begin replaying events of the past in our minds, wishing we had made better choices.
- **Letting Go** – We know we can't change the past and therefore accept it, making personal changes that can ensure a bright future.

Emotional problems come when we get stuck in our hurt by refusing to move past the event by letting go—the last stage. We refuse to forgive the person for what they've done to us. This unforgiving spirit begins to rule us and causes us to move to the next stage.

Rebellion

Tony broke the rules that were put in place to control his behavior. He rebelled against his dad. I've heard a great formula that describes this: Rules Without Relationship = Rebellion. This is so true! When we rebel, we begin acting out in anger to hurt the other person. We're even willing to experience further pain ourselves if we know we're hurting the person who has brought us pain. Do you remember the story of the two shop owners? One was willing to suffer to inflict pain on his rival. This is self-destructive behavior. We move to the next stage.

Unhealthy Relationships

Tony found people who would accept him, people who were just like him. Unfortunately, he formed relationships that encouraged him to continue to have the same bitter feelings. This led to further problems. Because we still need relationships, we find others who reinforce our point of view to make us feel better about our decisions. We need to know something about the type of person we befriend. They're also looking for our approval of their bad behavior. We find ourselves in very unhealthy relationships that encourage further emotional failure. The final stage follows.

Destruction/Death

Tony and his friends became very destructive, wanting to inflict pain on others. Our bitterness leads us to act out though destructive behavior. We do this to get the attention of the one who has hurt us. Our resentment turns into hate, which brings about a desire to inflict pain. Hate, taken to the extreme, is aggressive action. It's destructive. This can be the destruction of a relationship, physical harm that can lead to the death of another person, or physical harm that can lead to our death (suicide). This isn't what God wants! This is what Satan wants. He works to bring death while God works to bring life and peace. Paul writes that "the mind of sinful man is death, but the mind controlled by the Spirit is life and peace..." (Romans 8:6). God can win and give you the peace you're looking for if you allow Him to enter your mind and heart.

Ridding Myself of Bitterness

What do we do to rid ourselves of the bitterness that rules over us? What can we do to keep ourselves from falling into this trap? There must be something we can do. After all, the Bible instructs us to "get rid of all bitterness..." (Ephesians 4:31). There are some steps we can take:

Confess to God that we are responsible for our bitterness

Remember, no one can make us bitter. We make ourselves bitter. We must open up (become transparent) and acknowledge that we've chosen to become bitter. Take ownership of who you've become.

Confess to God that we have been unwilling to forgive

Unforgiveness is the cause of bitterness. Confession acknowledges to God we understand why we have become bitter. We now have pointed out the root of the problem. This leads to the next step.

Practice Forgiveness

Peter and Jesus had a conversation about forgiveness. The Bible teaches,

Then Peter came to Jesus and asked, "Lord, how many times shall I forgive my brother when he sins against me? Up to seven times?" Jesus answered, "I tell you, not seven times, but seventy-seven times."

Matthew 18:21-22

That's a lot of forgiveness! C. S. Lewis put it this way: "We find that the work of forgiveness has to be done over and over again. We forgive, we mortify our resentment; a week later some chain of thought carries us back to the original offence and we discover the old resentment blazing away as if nothing had been done about it at all. We need to forgive our brother seventy times seven not only for 490 offenses but for one offence."[49] How true this is. Satan wants us to rehash old painful memories. The key to overcoming the temptation to become bitter all over again is to practice forgiveness again. We forgive out of love. Our forgiving others is evidence we know God's love. God wants me to love and Satan wants to stop me. I should follow God's plan, not Satan's. So what's the difference? Check out the chart below:

God's Plan

- Focus on the good (what is done right).
- Know the truth (I am responsible for my emotions).
- Be in control (know that God loves me).
- Continue on the right path (focus on what is ahead of me).
- Care about others (be godly).
- Be kind (behave in a way that is helpful).
- Love (forgive and refuse to hold a grudge. Experience peace and joy).

Satan's Plan

- Focus on the bad (what is done wrong).
- Believe a lie (it's their fault).
- Be out of control (live to be loved by others).
- Get off course (focus on what is behind me).
- Care only about myself (be worldly).
- Seek revenge (behave in a way that is harmful).

- Be bitter/hateful (be unforgiving and hold a grudge. Experience disorder and evil).

Do the indicators reveal you're bitter? Have you made it through the grieving process successfully? Are stuck in "hurt" because of an unwillingness to forgive others for past mistakes? Is it leading to the death of your relationships? Do you find yourself in the center of Satan's plan? It's time to rid yourself of bitterness through confession and forgiveness. It's not God's choice. It's not the choice of the person who acted foolishly. It's your choice! Why don't you do it right now!

Dear God,
Help me let go of my past. I ask You to give me the strength to forgive those who have harmed me through the power of Your love. Please use my loving words and actions to change their hearts. Show them their need for You.

Chapter Ten

Up—Not Down: Overcoming Depression

I well remember them, and my soul is downcast within me.

Lamentations 3:20

Are you easily discouraged? Do you feel overwhelmed by your circumstances? You're not alone. Depression doesn't discriminate. It affects people of every color, race, economic status, age, and career—even ministers!

I live my life in a Catch-22. The choice is to please God or please people. Occasionally, I can accomplish both at the same time. Life is good! But there are moments when I have to choose between the two. I love to please people. After all, it's really nice to be liked. I also know I need to please God because His opinion is the only one that matters. It's easy to forget this and allow the wishes of people to influence us in the wrong way. Fortunately, because of my commitment to follow Him as I lead, I've been able to stick to His course and weather the storms. There have been storms and they haven't been easy times for me.

I've learned when people aren't "pleased" they tend to have an opinion about my leadership that's—how can I say this?—not very flattering. Welcome to the life of a pastor! I tend to take things to heart, and many times I find it hard to move past them. When this happens, depression sets in. For some crazy reason, I've had the false expectation that when people don't agree with me, they should be nice. Wouldn't it be awesome if that were true?

I don't like being in this condition. The way to get out of it is to change my mind. Have you heard that somewhere before? Overcoming depression is like overcoming other harmful emotions. It's a mind thing.

We learn about depression in particular from one of the prophets of God named Jeremiah. There's an awesome passage of Scripture that gives much insight into the condition of depression. Jeremiah was downcast. He was thinking about the fall of Jerusalem, which had occurred, and these thoughts discouraged him. He wrote about his feelings, the cause of his saddened mood, and the solution to his problem. Don't you want to know what he wrote? Here it is:

> I have been deprived of peace; I have forgotten what prosperity is. So I say, "My splendor is gone and all that I had hoped from the LORD." I remember my affliction and my wandering, the bitterness and the gall. I well remember them, and my soul is downcast within me. Yet this I call to mind and therefore I have hope: Because of the LORD'S great love we are not consumed, for his compassions never fail. They are new every morning; great is your faithfulness. I say to myself, "The LORD is my portion; therefore I will wait for him." The LORD is good to those whose hope is in him, to the one who seeks him; it is good to wait quietly for the salvation of the LORD.
>
> Lamentations 3:17-26

His depression happened because of the focus of his mind. When he changed his mind, his emotions also changed. Did you catch what he wrote? I love this phrase: "Yet this I call to mind..." He deliberately put the things of God in his head and it changed him. This gives me hope!

Jeremiah was down because he was remembering the affliction he suffered. It's almost as if he was measuring his success by the circumstances that were happening to him. As we've learned, our success is not dependent upon circumstances; it's dependent upon our relationship with God and our living up to His purposes. To think that circumstances can give true meaning to life is a false expectation. I must deliberately call some things to my mind—truth! I need to have realistic expectations about life and what's happening around me. If I don't—get ready for deep depression! Let's learn about the false expectations that cause us emotional trouble.

The Power of Unrealistic Expectations

Unrealistic expectations set us up to experience depression. Don Colbert, in his book *Stress Less,* writes that "a great deal of frustration does not arise from real situations that thwart us or keep us from finding the joy we desire. Rather, it arises from distortional expectations. In other words, we develop a 'distorted view' of what life should be like or should produce."[50]

Our minds can be programmed by the world's philosophy or by God's philosophy. There's a great difference between the two. Our thinking is affected in a great way by our senses, especially by what we see and what we hear. If we see things that are false or if we listen to people tell us false things, we begin believing things that aren't true and having unrealistic expectations. Bob George states that, "these expectations arise when we don't face life as it really is, but instead look at life and people as we think they should be."[51] There are some examples of unrealistic expectations in the Bible.

Unrealistic Expectation #1 – I Will Be Accepted and Not Rejected

This is the unrealistic expectation of acceptance. To think that everyone will like us is unrealistic. There's a difference between like and love. People can love us without liking us. Cain was loved by God, but he experienced rejection from God. We see this through the offering Cain and Abel gave to God. The Bible teaches,

> ...The LORD looked with favor on Abel and his offering, [5]but on Cain and his offering he did not look with favor. So Cain was very angry, and his face was downcast. [6]Then the LORD said to Cain, "Why are you angry? Why is your face downcast? [7]If you do what is right, will you not be accepted? But if you do not do what is right, sin is crouching at your door; it desires to have you, but you must master it.
>
> Genesis 4:4-7

Cain had a false belief that God would accept him even if he did what was wrong. His disappointment over the unrealistic expectation of being accepted caused him to be depressed. It's easy for us to experience the same thing. Check out this passage found in the fictional book titled *The Wisdom Hunter* by Randall Arthur. I love this!

> An old pastor asked, "How many people do you feel should like you? If the whole world liked you, would you like yourself? Nobody is accepted by everybody. Nobody, not beauty queens, movie stars, not even the Lord Jesus. On the other hand, nobody is rejected by

everybody either. Not the poorest man, not the ugliest man. Not the meanest man. Not even the devil.' With the chalk the old pastor scattered several dots around the circumference of the circle. 'Imagine these dots represent the billions of people living on earth. No matter where people stand on life's circle, it is the same: They have people to the left of them; they have people to the right of them. They have people who find them innocent; they have people who find them guilty. They have people who praise them; they have people who criticize them. No matter if a person changes his body shape, changes his atti-tude, changes his personality, changes his ideology, changes his public status—no matter where he repo-sitions himself on the circle, he will still get it from the left and the right. We need to accept where God has put us on the circle. We need to accept the body God has given us. We need to accept the many strong points God has blessed us with. If we accept who we are—we will not deny it when other people accept us, when people say they are our friends. However, the most important thing is not whether people accept or reject us; but whether God accepts or rejects us. And He accepts everyone who receives His Son Jesus Christ.'"[52]

That's good stuff!

Unrealistic Expectation #2 – Everyone Will Agree with Me and Not Ridicule Me

This is the unrealistic expectation of peace. Listen again to Jeremiah's words. He writes, "I have been deprived of peace, I have forgotten what prosperity is..." (Lamentations

3:17). Peace comes when we all agree. Friction comes when we have differing points of view. The Psalmist writes,

> My bones suffer mortal agony as my foes taunt me, saying to me all day long, "Where is your God?" Why are you downcast, O my soul? Why so disturbed within me? Put your hope in God, for I will yet praise him, my Savior and my God.
>
> Psalm 42:10-11

He was placing his hope in people and became depressed when they were being mean to him. He had an unrealistic expectation that they would agree with him. Instead, they were saying bad things about him and he became depressed because of his false belief. Wake up and smell the Cinnabon (coffee just doesn't do it anymore)! The fact is people will say bad things about us, especially if they don't agree with us. It's unrealistic to think everyone will agree with us. If you keep falling for this. it will drive you mad! Believe me—I know.

Unrealistic Expectation #3 – Everyone Will Treat Me with Respect and Not Harm Me

This is the unrealistic expectation of comfort. People will do foolish things that will affect us in negative ways. We read a passage that relates to this in the previous chapter on bitterness. The Bible teaches that "a foolish son brings grief to his father and bitterness to the one who bore him" (Proverbs 17:25). The father in this Scripture is affected emotionally because of an unrealistic expectation that people will not do things to harm us. Wouldn't it be great to live in a world where our children never did anything that affected us in a negative way? That's just not life. Because some can't come to grips with this, they become bitter over the bad behavior of their children or others, a bitterness that can lead to depression if they allow it to stick around.

Unrealistic Expectation #4 – I Will Experience Pleasure and Not Pain

This is the unrealistic expectation of happiness. Those who feel this way have an unrealistic expectation that they can make it through life finding happiness through pleasure and by avoiding pain. We don't always experience pleasure and there is pain. This search for happiness through pleasure comes from a selfish heart. They look for happiness through means other than God. They look for it through money, drugs, alcohol, appearance, fame, career, and sexual relationships. Although they find momentary gratification through these short-lived pleasurable experiences, they don't find happiness that is sustained.

Some, even in our youth culture, believe that sex is the answer. *USA Today* highlighted a study that links teen sexual intercourse with depression and suicide attempts. The Heritage Foundation discovered these connections are particularly true for young girls. According to their research, approximately twenty-five percent of sexually active girls say they are depressed all, most, or a lot of the time. This compares to eight percent of girls who are not sexually active who say they feel the same.[53] If you listen to those who follow the world's philosophy of "if it feels good, do it," you would think these sexually active girls would be happy. The study shows that pursuing pleasure doesn't make us happier; it makes us more depressed.

Jesus teaches that we can't have two masters. He says, "No one can serve two masters. Either he will hate the one and love the other, or he will be devoted to the one and despise the other. You cannot serve both God and Money" (Matthew

6:24). We don't find true happiness through money; we find it through knowing and serving God.

The expectation of happiness sets us up for great disappointment. There are a large number of depressed people in our society who've bought into this unrealistic expectation. J. P. Moreland and Laus Issler teach about this in their book, *Lost Virtue of Happiness*. They write, "When people live for pleasurable satisfaction, they become empty selves and, because God did not make us to live for 'happiness,' our lives fall apart."[54] They included the findings of a researcher named Seligman who spent his career studying happiness. They write,

> In the late 1980's, he noted that with the baby boom generation, American experience a tenfold increase in depression compared to earlier generations. If any condition increases this much in the span of a generation, we are safe to say an epidemic has occurred. A cause and cure must be sought…. He claimed that the cause of this epidemic was the fact that baby boomers stopped imitating their ancestors and seeking daily to live for a cause bigger than they—God, family, one's country—and instead spent from morning to night trying to live for themselves and their own pleasurable satisfaction. It is clear that such a strategy brings depression, not pleasure—or much else.[55]

Psychiatrist Juliet Schor, author of *Born to Buy: The Commercialized Child and the New Consumer Culture*, has discovered that involvement with the consumer culture contributes to anxiety, illness, and depression in some children. Schor sums up the message commercialized children receive: "They're more likely to have poor self-esteem, which is not a surprise because a lot of the messages the consumer culture sends them are that you're nobody if you don't have the right tennis shoes or you're not drinking the right soft drink."[56]

Life isn't about the pursuit of happiness; it's about the pursuit of joy. What's the difference? Happiness is connected with the physical feeling of euphoria. Joy is connected with adding value to others. Those who live for happiness set themselves up for disappointment and depression because life is not always pleasurable. Those who live for joy set themselves up for good emotional health because they know they can experience it by adding value to others even in the face of trouble. They accomplish this because their sense of fulfillment doesn't come from their circumstances. Their sense of fulfillment comes from trusting in God in the midst of their circumstances.

They Are Not in Control of You!

No one controls our thoughts but us. However, others affect our thinking. They affect the way we think when we believe negative things they've said about us. Unfortunately, it is easy to put more value on what others say about us than what we say to ourselves. This may sound like a selfish statement, but it really isn't. We should tell ourselves that our value comes from being a special creation of God. People didn't create us; God created us, so therefore we should not allow others to create false thoughts within our minds about our value. We shouldn't allow them to mold us into the image of the world; instead, we should allow God to mold us into the image of Christ.

You may have heard the statement before that joy comes from living by the following acrostic: J.O.Y. = Jesus, others, and yourself. This is absolutely true when it's attached to the priorities of our service. We should serve Christ by serving others. We do this by putting ourselves last. This happens when we have the heart of God, the heart of sacrifice. After all, God's purpose for us is to serve others sacrificially. This acrostic is not true as it connects to the way we think. The priority list should be as follows—God, ourselves, and others. It's the G.O.O. principle. I know that sounds silly. It's not a very good acrostic, but it contains great truth that can change unhealthy emotions. We are to think of God, our Creator. We are to place value on what God thinks about us first. Secondly, we are to see ourselves through the eyes of God. We are special in His sight. Therefore, we need to think of ourselves, knowing that God's opinion of us matters most. We are then to place value on the opinions of others, as they give us information about who we are. The measurement for our listening to them is simple. We must answer two questions:

- Are they encouraging us to see we are valuable creations of God?
- Are they encouraging us to become more like Christ?

People who place value on the opinion of others for their self-worth tend to tear others down in order to elevate their own standing. Get this—we are all equal and nothing we say about others or do to others will ever change that fact. God loves all of us the same. We become more emotionally healthy when we stop competing with one another and start helping each other find value from God. Are you attempting to find value through your status? It's "Stop Therapy" time. Stop having those thoughts! Stop believing that your value comes from people! Stop it right now! Put new information into your mind. Think these thoughts:

- God loves me not because of what I've done, but because of who I am.

- God has created me for a purpose—to love the love-able and the unlovable.
- I am of worth, not because of what people say or do to me, but because of what God says to me and does for me. He tells me He loves me and He has shown His love through the sacrifice of His Son, Jesus Christ.
- I will be joyful when people are rude because I know their negative behavior is a cry for help. God has ordained this moment to use me as His agent of love.

Putting this information into our minds helps us break the pattern of depression. It's time to take a look at that pattern and see how God can bring healing.

The Pattern Depression Follows

Depression follows a worldly pattern and Satan wants us to follow it. Let's look again at the words of Jeremiah. He writes, "I remember my affliction and my wandering, the bitterness and the gall. I well remember them, and my soul is downcast within me" Lamentations 3:19-20). There are some key words used in this passage that reveal the pattern that leads to depression. It begins with the words *affliction* and *wandering*. For our purposes, let's look at *wandering* first. We see the progression in the illustration below.

The Progression of Depression

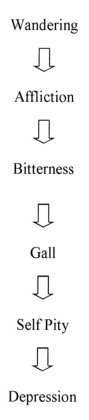

Wandering

⇩

Affliction

⇩

Bitterness

⇩

Gall

⇩

Self Pity

⇩

Depression

Wandering

Our minds get off course. We fall victim to unrealistic expectations and begin believing false things about life (Lamentations 3:19).

Affliction

We experience rejection, ridicule, disrespect, or pain (Lamentations 3:19).

Bitterness

We experience disappointment because of unmet expectations and we do not move past the hurt (Lamentations 3:19).

Gall

We become angry (Lamentations 3:19).

Self-Pity

We begin feeling sorry for ourselves (Lamentations 3:19). Jeremiah says, "I will remember my affliction…" The key words are *I* and *my*. His attention was on himself.

Depression

We begin to self-destruct (Lamentations 3:20). Our lives begin to change in a negative way.

The Effects of Depression

Once depression takes hold, it affects every part of life that defines us. The pattern leads to further difficulties. We can be described in the following ways:

- *Emotionally* – We experience fear, anger, worry, and sadness.

- *Mentally* – We have unrealistic expectations about what has happened, what is happening, or what will happen.
- *Socially* – We no longer enjoy being around others, and we withdraw.
- *Physically* – We begin to have problems with eating and sleeping. Our depression can lead to further sickness and cause us to lose our sexual desire.
- *Spiritually* – We become preoccupied with self, disobey God, lose hope, and lose our desire to live.

This sounds like a miserable life! So let's break the pattern. We need to learn how to be free. If depression follows a pattern, the way to end depression is to break the pattern.

Breaking the Pattern of Depression

Just as we followed some steps to rid ourselves of bitterness, there are some steps we can take to be healed of depression. When we accomplish the first step, the next two automatically occur.

Deliberately Change My Thinking

We see evidence of this taking place in Jeremiah's life. Look again at what he writes: "Yet this I call to mind and therefore I have hope…" (Lamentations 3:21). Depression begins with our wandering minds. To change the pattern, we must change our thinking by calling new things to mind— the truth. Do you remember what Paul teaches? He writes, "Do not conform any longer to the pattern of this world, but be transformed by the renewing of your mind. Then you will be able to test and approve what God's will is—his good, pleasing and perfect will" (Romans 12:2). We need to renew our minds. Those who are depressed need to follow the instruction given earlier. We are to manifest in a positive way about our future, seeing ourselves finding value from God, not from the comments or actions of those we know.

This might surprise you, but scientific research is focusing on the relationship between mental health and religion. Time magazine reports that "religious people are less depressed, less anxious and less suicidal than nonreligious people."[57] Michael McCullough, an associate professor of psychology and religious studies at the University of Miami, writes that "even if you compare two people who have symptoms of depression, the more religious person will be a little less sad." The article went on to reveal that "studies show that the more a believer incorporates religion into daily living, attending services, reading Scripture, and praying the better off he or she appears to be on two measures of happiness: frequency of positive emotions and overall sense of satis-faction with life."[58] This is amazing! Scientists have figured out the more we think about God, the better our emotions become.

We need to transform our minds. To transform our minds, we must change our unrealistic expectations into realistic ones. What are they?

- Realistic Expectation #1 – There will be moments when I'll be rejected.
- Realistic Expectation #2 – There will be moments when people will disagree with me and ridicule me.
- Realistic Expectation #3 –There will be moments when I will not be treated with respect and will be harmed.
- Realistic Expectation #4 – I will experience joy when I face trouble if I place my trust in God.
- Realistic Expectation #5 – God will never stop loving me because He is faithful.

Jeremiah writes, "Because of the LORD'S great love we are not consumed, for his compassions never fail. They are new every morning; great is your faithfulness" (Lamentations 3:22-23). Believing this truth about God really does affect our emotional health. This belief leads to the fulfillment of the second step.

Become Faithful

Remember, our emotions follow our thinking. How many times am I going to write this? You should really have it down by the time you finish reading this book! It's "Jeremiah Time" again. He writes, "I say to myself, "The LORD is my portion; therefore I will wait for him" (Lamentations 3:24). When God becomes my portion, He becomes my reason for being. When this is true, I'm faithful to wait on Him. I follow His instructions. I'm obedient. I break the pattern of wrong thinking, which results in right behavior. I don't live to control circumstances to become happy; I live to honor God, knowing He loves me and will care for me. This leads to the third step—my proper emotional response.

Respond With Hope

We've learned there are two emotions that deal with our future—discouragement and hope. God wants us to have hope. That Jeremiah guy really had a lot to say, so let's take a look once again at his words: "Yet this I call to mind and therefore I have hope... The LORD is good to those whose hope is in him, to the one who seeks him..." (Lamentations 3:21, 25). If he can have hope, so can you and so can I. No situation should get me down because I know the One who gives hope is with me.

Have you been struggling with depression? It's time to break the pattern! It's time to be transformed by the renewing of your mind.

God,
I confess I have failed because of my unrealistic expectations. Help me to have realistic expectations and to know the truth that You love me and will meet my every need. I give up my depression right now and claim the hope that comes in knowing You.

Chapter Eleven

It's About the Joy: God's Favorite Emotion

The prospect of the righteous is joy, but the hopes of the wicked come to nothing.

Proverbs 10:28

What have been the happiest moments of your life? Was it graduating from high school or college? Maybe it was landing your first job. What about your first kiss? The married amongst us can't forget about the big wedding day. Then there are those with kids. A birthday is a pretty big moment. When I look back on my life, I can say that all of these were happy times. I've noticed something, though—life isn't full of these moments. There are good days and there are bad days; there is ecstasy and there is pain. There must be more. Can happiness really be what life is all about?

Many live their lives in the same way by looking for happiness. In fact, they measure their success by it and place their trust in what they believe will bring them the happiness they're looking for. Some have come to understand there should be a second pursuit—the pursuit of joy. Charlotte Davis Kasl, who holds a Ph.D. and is an expert in the area of joy from a secular perspective, writes that "we are all born with a capacity for love and joy."[59] Good news, right? She also writes that "our culture may fear joy, because joy empowers people to feel alive, exuberant, self-respecting, and unlikely to tolerate being exploited or harmed."[60] Pretty awesome stuff! Don't you want to feel alive and exuberant? I must disagree with the last part of her statement. Those who are joyful do tolerate being harmed and exploited. Their joy is not dependent on the treatment they receive from people. The joyful go on the offensive when harmed and exploited in an effort to bring change to the heart of the aggressor. They want the person who harmed or exploited them to experience the joy that comes from knowing and trusting in God.

We learned in the chapter on depression that there's a difference between happiness and joy. We discovered that happiness often comes from pleasure. We use one to get the other. Pleasure is a physiological feeling while happiness is a psychological feeling. There's a problem with pleasurable experiences—they're temporary and don't last. People who believe life is about happiness pursue pleasure and become very disillusioned about their life when pleasure can't be maintained. The pleasure high always ends. Pleasure in and of itself is not a bad thing. The danger comes when we live for it and become addicted to it. We become very self-involved, looking only to the next source of a "feel-good" experience. We become the center of our world and, because of this, people seek pleasure through means other than God.

Trusting in the material doesn't satisfy us and leaves us wanting for more. Brad Pitt, the famous actor, was interviewed in *Rolling Stone* magazine about his role in the movie *Fight Club*. The movie is about a man who lives looking for satisfaction. Pitt made these comments:

> Man, I know all these things are supposed to seem important to us—the car, the condo, our version of success—but if that's the case, why is the general

feeling out there reflecting more impotence and isolation and desperation and loneliness? If you ask me, I say toss all this—we gotta find something else. Because all I know is that at this point in time, we are heading for a dead end, a numbing of the soul, a complete atrophy of the spiritual being. And I don't want that.

The interviewer asked, "So if we're heading toward this kind of existential dead end in society, what do you think should happen?" Pitt answered,

Hey, man, I don't have those answers yet. The emphasis now is on success and personal gain. I'm sitting in it, and I'm telling you, that's not it. I'm the guy who's got everything. I know. But I'm telling you, once you've got everything, then you're just left with yourself. I've said it before and I'll say it again: it doesn't help you sleep any better, and you don't wake up any better because of it.[61]

Many come to the conclusion, like Pitt, that there must be more. Some secular psychologists agree. Ed Diener, a psychologist at the University of Illinois, says that "materialism is toxic for happiness."[62] How true this is!

Experts from other religious backgrounds also understand our desire to find real meaning and joy in life. Osho, a philosopher who uses thought from Eastern religion and connects it with technology and Western science, gives his own perspective in his book called *Joy: The Happiness That Comes from Within.* He writes, "Happiness is unbelievable. It seems that man cannot be happy. If you talk about your depression, sadness, misery, everybody believes it; it seems natural. If you talk about your happiness nobody believes you—it seems unnatural."[63] He went on to teach about Sigmund Freud and his feelings about happiness. He wrote that Freud "after forty years of research into the human mind—working with thousands of people, observing thousands of disturbed minds—came to the conclusion that happiness is a fiction: Man cannot be happy. At the most, we can make things a little more comfortable, that's all. At the most we can reduce unhappiness a little, that's all, but happy? Man cannot be."[64] From these statements we see that people who buy into the world's philosophy are learning that living for happiness is a shallow existence.

Osho also writes about the idea of pleasure. He teaches that "pleasure keeps you in a neurotic state, restless, always in turmoil. So many desires, and every desire unquenchable, clamoring for attention. You remain a victim of a crowd of insane desires—insane because they are unfulfillable—and they go on dragging you in different directions."[65] This is the human predicament. Many seek pleasure in the hopes it will give their life value only to discover that it falls short of that goal.

Adam and Eve discovered this. They bought into the lie from Satan that pleasure was the path of life. The Bible says,

> When the woman saw that the fruit of the tree was good for food and pleasing to the eye, and also desirable for gaining wisdom, she took some and ate it. She also gave some to her husband, who was with her, and he ate it. Then the eyes of both of them were opened, and they realized they were naked; so they sewed fig leaves together and made coverings for themselves.
>
> Genesis 3:6-7

They saw the fruit was good for food and pleasing to the eye. That must have been one fine-looking piece of fruit. Let the food problems begin! Think about what happened after the "big bite." You know, when they chomped down. They became very self-conscious after they chose pleasure over being obedient to God. They realized they were naked and made the first "Adam and Eve Hilfiger" swimwear.

The search for pleasure, taken to the extreme, results in addictive behavior. Author and psychologist Robert A. Johnson writes about this problem in his book, *Ecstasy: Understanding the Psychology of Joy*:

It is the great tragedy of contemporary Western society that we have virtually lost the ability to experience the transformative power of ecstasy and joy... We seek ecstasy everywhere, and for a moment we think we have found it. But, on a very deep level, we remain unfulfilled... Our spirits need nourishment as much as ever. But, having excluded the inner experience of divine ecstasy from our lives, we can look only for its physical equivalent. And no matter how hard we look, or how many low-grade ecstatic experiences we accumulate, we crave more. This craving has led to the most characteristic symptom of our time: addictive behavior... Addiction is the negative side of spiritual seeking. We are looking for an exultation of the spirit; but instead of fulfillment we get a short-lived physical thrill that can never satisfy the chronic, gnawing emptiness with which we are beset.[66]

He also writes the following about our craving for the material in this world:

Even the clothes we wear tell us something is amiss. Both men and women today "dress for success" by wearing ties—in effect separating their heads, their thinking processes, from the rest of their bodies and thus symbolically cutting off sensation below their necks. When they take their ties off at the end of the day they go wild. All that bottled-up sensation comes rushing out looking for somewhere to go.[67]

Pleasure is not the answer. There must be something more. Humanity has been searching for that "something" for our entire existence. What is it? We've learned that those who live for happiness live for pleasure. There's something else: It's joy!

In an article in *Christian History Magazine* titled "Ministries of Mercy: Mother Teresa," Ruth A. Tucker writes the following:

> Mother Teresa was sometimes challenged about the long-term effects of her humanitarian ministry. For example, she was asked, "Why give people fish to eat instead of teaching them how to fish?" She had a quick response: "But my people can't even stand. They're sick, crippled, demented. When I have given them fish to eat and they can stand, I'll turn them over and you give them the rod to catch the fish." She was quick to emphasize, however, that she gave people more than "fish." Equally important was that which came from the heart—love and joy. The poor, she insisted, deserve more than just service and dedication: "If our actions are just useful actions that give no joy to the people, our poor people would never be able to rise up to the call which we want them to hear, the call to come closer to God. We want to make them feel that they are loved."[68]

We need joy! Remember, pleasure is a physiological feeling and happiness is a psychological feeling. Joy is a spiritual feeling. It's an emotion that is spiritual in nature. Once again, people who follow a worldly philosophy understand the nature of joy. Check out more of what Osho writes. He teaches that joy "is different, totally different from pleasure or happiness. It has nothing to do with the outside, with the other; it is an inner phenomenon. Joy is not dependent on circumstances; it is your own. ...It is a state of peace."[69]

How do we experience this joy? I'd like to attempt to answer that question. Let's begin by reading a passage of Scripture written by Paul to the church at Thessalonica: "Be joyful always; pray continually; give thanks in all circumstances, for this is God's will for you in Christ Jesus" (1 Thessalonians 5:16-18). We're commanded to be joyful always. If this is a command, then it's an expectation. Not only can we experience it, but we're also expected to experience it.

Why is it so important for us to be joyful always? This is an important question. We've learned our emotions affect every part of our lives that define us. The same is also true of joy. It makes living an awesome experience, not something to dread. Let's take a look at the effects of joy.

How Joy Affects Life

Joy does affect every area that defines us. Below is information on how joy affects each specifically.

Emotionally

Our emotions are constructive and not destructive. We know we experience emotional failure when we harm ourselves and others. God's created us to add value to others. We experience joy when we are used by God to benefit humanity.

Mentally

We think correct thoughts that lead to right behaviors. We've learned our emotions follow our thoughts. If our thoughts are right, our emotions will be correct. We know with our minds that the first pursuit of life is joy, not happiness.

Socially

We're the right example for others to follow. Because we're emotionally responding in the right way, we're encouraging others to do the same. This is a form of servanthood. We serve others by properly showing them how to live, which strengthens relationships. We experience joy when there is peace in our relationships, a peace that comes from mutual respect and a desire to be used to help others succeed.

Physically

We're in the best possible physical condition. This is due to the absence of stress. Removing stress changes our attitude. Having joy transforms us from a negative and pessimistic person to one who is optimistic and positive. *General Psychiatry* magazine included a study that was performed on one thousand people aged 65-85 that revealed the positive effect attitude plays in physical health. Researchers discovered after nearly ten years of follow-up that those who considered themselves to be optimistic had a fifty-five percent lower risk of death from all causes and had a twenty-three percent lower risk of heart-related death. The study indicated that optimistic people drink and smoke less, are more physically active, and cope with stress more effectively.[70] It all starts with joy!

Spiritually

We're at peace because of our complete faith in God. The result of my trust in God is living my life in a joyful spiritual state. I don't trust in worldly elements for happiness; I trust in God for my joy. Remember, joy comes from our spirituality. My life is not in turmoil because I don't trust in my circumstances for my sense of importance. I'm valuable because God loves me. He's committed to meeting my every need.

This lifestyle just absolutely sounds fantastic to me. What about you? Can you imagine living your life in this way? This is God's expectation for us. Yes—expectation! Those who are living for pleasure and happiness don't know what they're missing. So how do I add joy to my life?

Adding Joy

We can take steps toward experiencing joy. They include the following:

Completely Trust in God

Trust must be complete. We can't maintain control of some areas while giving God control of others. Joy is spiritual. I must be completely devoted to God to experience it. Our devotion affects us. Paul writes, "May the God of hope fill you with all joy and peace as you trust in him, so that you may overflow with hope by the power of the Holy Spirit" (Romans 15:13). If you have a pen or pencil, underline the phrase "as you trust in him." When we trust in God, we experience joy and peace, and hope overflows. He is our strength. We aren't discouraged when tough situations come our way because we know God is in control and He has a plan for us. We're reminded of God's promise found in Romans 8:28: "And we know that in all things God works for the good of those who love him, who have been called according to his purpose" (Romans 8:28). We completely trust in God when we believe this. God can't break this promise. It would violate His character.

My emotional problems stem from what I believe. If I believe that life is about happiness, then I try to control events in an effort to secure happiness. I'm not trusting in God; I'm trusting in my ability to control events to bring pleasure. If I trust in God, I don't allow my circumstances to rule over me. I can experience joy in the face of difficulties. Remember, joy is spiritual and the spiritual life is about the big "L" word. It's about love. It's the character of God. He's love! Since this is the case, I must know I'm loved by God and return that love to God to know what joy is. Don't miss this! There's no greater joy than to love and be loved. Do you remember reading some stuff out loud a while back? I have a great idea, let's do it again. Read this out loud: "There is no greater joy than to love and be loved!" I come to love God because of what I know and believe about Him. He's all about me. He cares about me. It's cool to be cared for. Because I'm loved by Him, I want to love Him. On a spiritual level I know the following things:

- I'm loved by God.
- I can trust God to meet my needs.
- God has a purpose for my life.
- God has a purpose for everything that happens to me and around me. Because of this, I can give thanks in all circumstances (1 Thessalonians 5:18).

This is truth. When I believe it, I experience peace in my mind and heart. My circumstances don't change these beliefs. This allows me to live a consistent life that's emotionally stable. God doesn't stop loving me and I don't stop loving Him just because my circumstances change.

I'm blown away by the attitude of Bethany Hamilton, a surfer who experienced joy in the midst of tragedy. Bethany was once ranked the best amateur teen surfer in Hawaii. In October of 2003, she was attacked by a tiger shark and lost her arm. As you can imagine, this was an unexpected and difficult circumstance to deal with. She could've allowed this to devastate her, but her response was quite different. She decided to turn this event into something positive. She *decided*! This was a deliberate choice. The attack became the catalyst for her performing some compassionate acts to help others who were hurting. She also hasn't lost her competitive spirit. In a story in *USA Today*, Jill Lieber writes,

> As always, Hamilton remains undaunted. She has told her father that if having only one arm proved detrimental to reaching the top in competitive surfing, then she'd see about playing soccer. Her pastor, Steve Thompson, said, "She's looking forward to the future. She's asking herself, 'How can I show the world I still have a life, that I enjoy my life, and that my life is filled with joy?' She has an underlying trust that God is taking care of her."[71]

The word *joy* just jumps off the page, doesn't it? She has joy because joy isn't controlled by circumstances. Are you getting this? Bethany is a great example of someone who is able to maintain a positive attitude and express healthy emotions because of her trust in God. Again, trust is the key to emotional health. To maintain my trust in God, I need to take another step.

Remain in Christ's Love

Not only do I need to remember that Christ loves me, but I need to remain in love with God. As long as I do, I experience emotional success. How do I remain in love with God? I need to love God like Jesus loves God. Jesus says,

As the Father has loved me, so have I loved you.
Now remain in my love. If you obey my commands,
you will remain in my love, just as I have obeyed my
Father's commands and remain in his love. I have
told you this so that my joy may be in you and that
your joy may be complete. My command is this:
Love each other as I have loved you.

John 15:9-12

This is great! Jesus told us how to have His joy and how
to complete our joy. We're to follow the command. The
command is to love each other as He has loved us. How
did He love us? He gave it up! What does that mean? He
sacrificed. He gave his life for us. He lived it for us, and
He allowed it to be taken away for us. Jesus cared more
for humanity than He did for His own life. He loved others
more than Himself. We'll know joy when we do the same.
He experienced joy because He knew his sacrifice made a
difference. Joy will well up in us when we know our sacrifice is making a difference. There is another step.

Think Like Jesus Thinks

I need to have a mind that is consistent with the mind
of Christ. Think about what Paul teaches: "We have not
received the spirit of the world but the Spirit who is from
God, that we may understand what God has freely given
us.... For who has known the mind of the Lord that he may
instruct him? But we have the mind of Christ" (1 Corinthians
2:12, 16). We've learned that the Holy Spirit is known as the
mind of Christ. I want to point out something it says. Paul
tells us what he does. He instructs us. He teaches us what
Jesus thinks. By speaking to us, he leads us to think like
Christ thinks. Here we go again. Don't get irritated by my
writing this yet again, but "our actions follow our thinking."

Since this is true, it just makes sense that we become like Christ when we think like Christ. Right? When we think like Christ thinks, we live like Christ lives.

God's Spirit influences us to be like Him. Don't miss this. It's one of those big statements that help us understand what God's up to. We need to remember that everything the Holy Spirit does He does to lead us to be love as Christ is love. It's seen through the fruits we bear. We begin bearing the fruits of God's spirit, seen in the life of Christ, when we think like Christ thinks and act like Jesus acts. The Bible says, "But the fruit of the Spirit is love, joy, peace, patience, kindness, goodness, faithfulness, gentleness and self-control. Against such things there is no law" (Galatians 5:22-23). This is awesome! I don't think it's by coincidence that these fruits are listed in the order they appear. First there is love and then there is joy which leads to patience, kindness, goodness, faithfulness, gentleness, and self-control. The final fruit is self-control. What's up with that?

Jesus' mind led Him to live a self-controlled life. It's all about attitude. We learn about Jesus' attitude through Paul's letter written to the church at Philippi. He writes,

Your attitude should be the same as that of Christ Jesus: Who, being in very nature God, did not consider equality with God something to be grasped, but made himself nothing, taking the very nature of a servant, being made in human likeness. And being found in appearance as a man, he humbled himself and became obedient to death — even death on a cross! Therefore God exalted him to the highest place and gave him the name that is above every name, that at the name of Jesus every knee should bow, in heaven and on earth and under the earth, and every tongue confess that Jesus Christ is Lord, to the glory of God the Father.

Philippians 2:5-11

Jesus is our example of how we should show our emotions. We've learned about anger, jealousy, pride, depression, bitterness, and anxiety. This passage reveals that Jesus mastered all. Because He did, He was a joyous man. Take a look at how He mastered His emotions to win over the temptation to blow His emotional life:

- **Jesus was not unholy in His anger; He was selfless.** The Scripture teaches us that He made Himself nothing (Philippians 2:7). I must have this attitude. As Christ was selfless, I will be selfless. I must think correctly. I must know the wellbeing of others is more important than my pain. Paul instructs, "Let us fix our eyes on Jesus, the author and perfecter of our faith, who for the joy set before him endured the cross, scorning its shame, and sat down at the right hand of the throne of God. Consider him who endured such opposition from sinful men, so that you will not grow weary and lose heart" (Hebrews 12:2-3).
- **Jesus was not jealous; He was obedient.** The Scripture teaches us that He was obedient to death (Philippians 2:8). I must have this attitude. As Christ was obedient, I'll be obedient to do whatever He asks. I need to think correctly. I must simply live up to the expectations of God—nothing more, nothing less. Living up to His expectations for my life should become my standard.
- **Jesus was not proud; He was humble.** The Scripture teaches us that He humbled himself and became a man (Philippians 2:8). I must have this attitude. As Christ was humble, I will be humble, becoming what-

ever God wants me to become. Jesus was willing to become a man and I must be willing to become ___. I don't know how you should fill in the blank. I have to be concerned about how I'm to fill in the blank. I believe God will let me know. I also believe He'll do the same for you. You'll do it when you're humble. I'll do it when I'm humble. I have to think correctly. My desire must be to become whatever God wants me to become, allowing Him to use my life to put His love on display. This is cool! I'm to be God's display board—a big advertisement for who He is and what He does. Sweet!

- **Jesus was not depressed; He was determined**. The Scripture reveals that He was willing to suffer (Philippians 2:8). He was willing to suffer and experience pain for a greater purpose. I must have this attitude: As Christ was determined, I will be determined to make it through hardships. I have to think correctly. I need to remember God has a purpose for all things in my life.

- **Jesus was not bitter; He was understanding**. The Scriptures reveal that Christ knew we needed to bring glory to God (Philippians 2:11). He knew we needed a Lord. I must have this attitude. As Christ was understanding, I will be understanding, expecting ungodly people to act in an ungodly manner. It's crazy to think ungodly people will act like God. That just doesn't make sense. That's bad thinking, which leads to false expectations, which leads to big-time disappointment. I have to change my thinking and think correctly. Here's the correct thought: I can't expect people to honor God until they know Him personally, a knowledge which comes through confessing Christ as their Savior and Lord.

- **Jesus was not anxious; He was trusting**. The Scripture teaches that Jesus was exalted (Philippians 2:9). Jesus knew God had a plan. I must have this attitude. As Christ was trusting, I will be trusting, knowing God cares for me and has a plan for my life. I have to think correctly! I need to remember God loves me, will meet my needs, has a purpose for my life, and has a purpose for the events of my life—to build my faith in Him or to use me to spread "the love." I know my emotions will waver if my trust in God falters. I can't let it falter! I must succeed! Don't let yours falter. Succeed!

Dear God,
Help me to have the mind of Christ. I ask You to help me become love as Christ is love. I ask You to turn my jealousy into obedience, my pride into humility, my depression into determination, my bitterness into understanding, and my anxiousness into trust. I look to You for my spiritual and emotional health and I commit myself to no longer look to people for my sense of purpose and happiness. Make my joy complete as I rely on You!

Chapter Twelve

Seize the Day:
The Successful Journey

> Be very careful, then, how you live—not as unwise
> but as wise, [16]making the most of every opportunity,
> because the days are evil.
>
> Ephesians 5:15-16

It's a daily thing. You know—life. It's full of choices that take us on a journey either closer to God or away from Him. The journey closer to Him brings more emotional stability every day. The journey away from Him just leads to more and more headache and heartache. It's a headache because my mind gets all screwed up, and it leads to heartache because I start believing junk that's not true. When this happens, I don't fulfill my purpose.

Every day is an opportunity for us to live up to our calling. We do this when we're emotionally smart, controlling our emotions for God's glory. Let's remember what we've learned. We've learned that God has called us to be love as He is love, a love which results in joy. We've also learned that the loving are people of sacrifice who reach out toward others and serve them to help improve their lives. We have opportunity each day to stay on course and accomplish this goal or to be derailed and self-destruct. God wants us to achieve the purpose of becoming love while Satan works really hard to distract us, to keep us from living up to our calling by messing with our emotions. We must seize the day!

You may have heard the phrase "Carpe Diem." It was made famous in the movie *Dead Poets Society*. It means to "seize the day." We seize the day when we make the most of every opportunity. Paul writes to the church of Ephesus these words: "Be very careful, then, how you live—not as unwise but as wise, making the most of every opportunity, because the days are evil" (Ephesians 5:15-16). To seize the day, we need to be wise and avoid what's evil. So what do the wise do? They trust in God. The unwise begin trusting in themselves, taking them on a ride—an emotional roller coaster. I've never liked roller coasters, but this one is the worst of all! Why? Because of the big fall! We fall away from living the good life. Since we are to make the most of every day, I want to share with you how we can do it.

Our success is dependent upon our daily choices. Erwin McManus, in his book *Seizing Your Diving Moment*, makes a great statement: "No matter what kind of life you've lived, no matter how many wrong choices you've made, the next moment is waiting to give birth to new life."[72] Is this good news or what? Do you believe it? This should give us great hope. With every choice we set our course. We turn our navigation knobs. You never know how one day will change your direction—for better or for worse. You may have had a very successful past, but a bad choice today can change your future in a negative way. Maurice Clarett understands that. He had a promising future ahead of him. He was a former standout college football star who was arrested for pulling a gun and robbing some people in an alley. He learned that one decision can set you on a negative course.

You may have had a difficult past, but a good choice today can change your present and your future in a positive way. Think about Rahab in the Bible. She also understood the importance of choices. She was a prostitute who became obedient to God by helping His servants in a time of need. This decision changed her life and her family's life. Her choice set her life in a new direction toward God. The choices we make each moment matter, and our emotions affect these choices. So where will your choices take you?

God has equipped us to make the right decisions, to put the right information in or minds, and to put the right beliefs in our hearts. We see a great example of the choices that we're to make daily in God's Word. Do you remember the story about the people of Israel who faced the decision about going into the Promised Land? They'd been rescued from captivity in Egypt by God and had made their way to the border of the Promised Land. They sent twelve spies in to check it out. Ten of them came back and gave a negative report, causing the people of Israel to choose not to enter. Their thinking affected their beliefs about the future. This choice not only affected them, but it also affected the people of Israel for the next forty years as they wandered in the wilderness. Later in the Scripture, we see the people of Israel once again standing on the border of the Promised Land after their time of wandering, preparing to go in. What will they do this time? God gives them instruction about the choices they are about to make:

See, I set before you today life and prosperity, death and destruction. For I command you today to love the LORD your God, to walk in his ways, and to keep his commands, decrees and laws; then you will live and increase, and the LORD your God will bless you in the land you are entering to possess. But if your heart turns away and you are not obedient, and if you are drawn away to bow down to other gods and worship them, I declare to you this day that you will certainly be destroyed. You will not live long in the land you are crossing the Jordan to enter and possess. This day I call heaven and earth as witnesses against you that I have set before you life and death, blessings and curses. Now choose life, so that you and your children may live and that you may love the LORD your God, listen to his voice, and hold fast to him. For the LORD is your life, and he will give you many years in the land he swore to give to your fathers, Abraham, Isaac and Jacob.

Deuteronomy 30:15-20

We learn some important lessons about making the most of the moment and the choices we make daily from this Scripture. Let's check them out!

The Choice: Today or Tomorrow

We seize the day when we live as if today was our last. I must decide if I'm going to live for today or for tomorrow. Will I make changes today to honor God or will I wait for tomorrow? God wants us to live for today. We hear the word *today* used two times in the Scripture from above. We read the phrase "See, I set before you today..." and the statement "I command you today." Have you noticed that not everyone lives for today? Some live for tomorrow and waste a good twenty-four hours that could have been used to do God's thing and not our own. This habit affects our lives. How?

Those Who Live for Tomorrow Wait

Do you find yourself saying, "I'll do that tomorrow"? What's wrong with today? We've learned there are three primary emotions—love, fear, and anger. The emotion that causes us to make the decision to wait is often the emotion of fear. We fear because of misplaced trust. If Satan can get us to trust in our ability and not God's, he'll stop us in our tracks. By influencing our source of trust, he causes us to wait. He loves this because he knows the longer we wait, the harder it is for us to take action.

We learned early in this book that it's important to give our lives to God—to make Him Lord. You may have the attitude of "I'll give my life to God tomorrow." I've got a question for you: What's wrong with today? You may choose not to do it today out of a fear you'll no longer be in control. In fact, when you give your life to God, you're out of control. This isn't a bad thing; it's a fantastic thing because you don't have to rely on your "imperfect self" to determine the best course. We rely on a perfect God who's not too distracted by evil to point the way. Satan wants you to fear being out of control. God wants you to know there's nothing to fear when He's in control.

You may have the attitude of "I'll serve God tomorrow." I've got a question for you: What's wrong with today? You may be afraid that people won't accept what you do for them and will respond in an unkind manner. This fear comes because we mistakenly believe our value comes from what people do or say to us. Stop it! That's just not true. You're afraid you'll be devalued, causing you to lose your happiness. The fear you feel in this situation is an indication you're not trusting in God for your sense of worth, which would lead to lasting joy. Don't you want joy?

You may also have the attitude of "I'll tell my friend about Jesus tomorrow." I have a question for you: What's wrong with today? The emotion of fear also rules in this situation. You become fearful you'll be rejected. This fear indicates you're more concerned about how people respond to you than what your message can do for them. If your message isn't accepted by others, it reveals the condition of their heart, not yours. Satan wants you to see their rejection as a personal attack. God wants you to see their rejection is a form of self-destruction. They're harming themselves, not you. Those who live for today don't live out of fear, which moves us away from others. They act very differently.

Those Who Live for Today Run

They're out of the blocks. They're moving. They're taking action. Something causes them to do this. It's a specific view about life. Our choices become more important when we begin to see the preciousness of life.

How would it affect your choices today if you knew you had only one day to live? To seize the day, to make the most of the moment, we should live as if today is our last day on earth. The Scripture teaches us, "Do not boast about tomorrow, for you do not know what a day may bring forth" (Proverbs 27:1) We're not promised tomorrow. I'm not saying that to scare you; I'm saying that because it's truth. James writes,

> Now listen, you who say, "Today or tomorrow we will go to this or that city, spend a year there, carry on business and make money." Why, you do not even know what will happen tomorrow. What is your life? You are a mist that appears for a little while and then vanishes.
>
> James 4:13-14

Erwin McManus told the story about Joe White, an evangelist who was diagnosed with terminal cancer. He grasped the truth of these words. When others talked with him about his cancer, he shared that he felt more fortunate than they were. You may wonder how in the world he could feel this way. He felt this way because he was clear that today might be the last day he had to live. He believed he had been given a gift—"the value of today."[73] We really have been given a gift—*today*!

What will you do with today? What should we do with today? Don't you wish someone would answer that question? This is your lucky day, as if there is anything such as luck. Let me rephrase this. This is the day God wants you to learn what you're to do with your day. I just have the privilege of pointing it out. Jesus answers the question for us: "But seek first his kingdom and his righteousness, and all these things will be given to you as well. Therefore do not worry about tomorrow, for tomorrow will worry about itself...." (Matthew 6:33-34). Today, we're to seek first His kingdom. We aren't to worry about tomorrow; we're to show God's love today. Love is the emotion that causes us to live for today. It motivates us. Love moves us toward others to make a positive impact.

The Choice: Risk or Safety

We seize the day when we seek to advance God's kingdom first (Matthew 6:33-34a). This should be our daily priority. We advance God's kingdom through obeying Him. Every day is filled with kingdom-advancing choices.

There are many people who want to build God's kingdom. In fact, I believe that a vast majority of people who claim to be Christians want to build His kingdom. They want to advance His causes. The question is do they want to do it first? Many seek to build their own kingdoms first and then advance God's. Out of pride, they feel their life is more valuable when they receive acclaim for what they have. Out of fear, they may be afraid to let go of their possessions. Letting go would cause them to feel out of control. They may think it's safer to take care of their own kingdom first. That's not the instruction given to us by Jesus. How do we know if we're interested in building our kingdoms first?

If we're interested in building our kingdoms first, we worry about tomorrow. Once again, fear has become our predominant emotion. We hold on to things today because of what we think they'll do for us tomorrow. It makes us feel safe to hold on to those things, fearing what life would be without them. Those things become our security blanket. This isn't God's plan. Let's take a look at the entire passage, reading what Jesus speaks to the people:

> And why do you worry about clothes? See how the lilies of the field grow. They do not labor or spin. Yet I tell you that not even Solomon in all his splendor was dressed like one of these. If that is how God clothes the grass of the field, which is here today and tomorrow is thrown into the fire, will he not much more clothe you, O you of little faith? So do not worry, saying, 'What shall we eat?' or 'What shall we drink?' or 'What shall we wear?' For the pagans run after all these things, and your heavenly Father knows that you need them. But seek first his kingdom and his righteousness, and all these things will be given to you as well. Therefore do not worry about tomorrow, for tomorrow will worry about itself. Each day has enough trouble of its own."
>
> Matthew 6:28-34

Did you catch the phrase—"For the pagans run after all these things..."? Those who are evil live to get these things and to hold on to them. Those who are godly live to please Him, knowing He will meet their needs. They release those things to help others. Making this choice requires us to take a risk. Taking this risk requires our trusting in someone else—God!

Those Who Choose to Risk Have Faith in God

We're willing to take a risk because of our trust in God. We've learned that faith in God is the source of our emotional health. Those who advance God's kingdom are willing to take risks, and they do so with confidence.

I don't know if you've figured this out yet, but the Christian life is about risk. John Piper, in his book *Don't Waste Your Life,* includes a quote by Stephen Neill. It highlights the attitude of Christians in the early church. He writes, "Every Christian knew that sooner or later he might have to testify to his faith at the cost of his life"[74] I wonder how many of us would be Christians today if we were faced with this risk. Would we choose safety instead? This reminds me of Esther in the Bible. When faced with the possibility of being put to death for approaching the king without permission in an effort to save God's people, she says, "If I perish, I perish" (Esther 4:16). What an amazing attitude to have. The great thing about her willingness to risk was what it led to. It advanced God's kingdom. She was willing to make this choice because she sought God's kingdom first, even if it meant giving her life.

Piper shared that Christians in the first three centuries of the church set the pattern of growth under threat. He writes that "it was the Christ –exalting love that the Christians showed in spite of risk that stunned the pagan world."[75] A really important lesson is learned from this statement. Our risk puts God's love on display. Taking the risk that our words and/or actions will be rejected shows our love for people. It lets them know they're worth the risk. This proves we care about them. We've learned about risk, but what about safety?

Those Who Choose Safety Have Faith in Themselves

There are those who opt for safety. Think about the people of Israel who left Egypt for the Promised Land. They were finally about to enter it. They had an opportunity forty years earlier, but while on the border of that land, they chose safety instead of risk. They said the people in the land were too great for them to overcome. This belief led to fear, the emotional reflex that came from their thinking. They trusted in what they could do alone and chose to protect themselves. Only two were willing to take the risk. Only two had right thoughts and right beliefs. They were excited about what God would do. They were confident in God, and it appears as though joy was their reflex emotion, the joy of knowing God would give them a great victory. They were the only two among the people who were blessed—the ones who were willing to advance God's kingdom first. Is this good stuff, or what? There is yet another choice.

The Choice: Life or Death

We seize the day when we choose life. According to the Scriptures, we can choose life or death. With life comes certain things, and with death comes certain things. The Scripture teaches, "See, I set before you today life and prosperity, death and destruction" (Deuteronomy 30:15). We also read these words: "This day I call heaven and earth as witnesses against you that I have set before you life and death, blessings and curses" (Deuteronomy 30:19).

The choices that were set before the people were "life," which brings prosperity and blessings or "death," which brings destruction and curses. Let me see here. I have a choice between prosperity and blessings or destruction and curses? What will I choose? That's a hard one. Yeah right! It's a no-brainer! Don't get confused about this. We're not to live our lives to receive prosperity and blessing—to attempt to manipulate God to get these things. If we did, we would be selfish people. Again, we've learned that we're not to live to be blessed; we're to live to be a blessing. Living to be a blessing in life gives us purpose. Our lives prosper when the lives of others are improved because of our influence. We have a sense of meaning and fulfillment. Meaning and fulfillment are blessings. We feel alive. Those who live to be blessed use other people. They don't add value to others; they take from them. They destroy them. This isn't our purpose. We feel empty and useless when we do this because we've caused harm to others. Feeling empty and useless is our curse. We feel a sense of darkness and discouragement.

God didn't choose life or death for the people; they made the choice for themselves. Now which sounds better to you? Life that brings prosperity and blessings or death that brings destruction and curses? It's your choice. God didn't choose for them, but He told them which one they should choose. The Scripture instructs us to "now choose life..." (Deuteronomy 30:19). When? Now! You can choose it right now. So how do we choose life? The Scripture answers this for us.

Those Who Choose Life Are Passionate About God

We're commanded to love the Lord our God (Deuteronomy 30:16). To be passionate about the Lord, He must be our God. We're always passionate about our God. Who is your God? This is a personal question. How would you fill in the blank? "I love the ____ my God." What goes in the blank? What are you passionate about? What do you desire? What do you trust in for your happiness? If it's not God, then you need a heart transformation. Your desires need to change. What about this desire thing?

Desire is not evil. We become evil when we have misdirected desires. Desire and passion go together. Those who aren't passionate live an empty life. They don't care about life. For life to have meaning, there must be passion. Our passion is our reason to exist. It's our reason to live. Our passion gives us life. McManus teaches that "when you are passionate about God, you can trust your passions. God uses our passions as a compass to guide us... When you are madly in love with God, you can do whatever you want."[76] This is true because our desires are His desires and there's no danger of doing what's wrong. We completely trust in Him and are at peace because He's our desire. The Psalmist writes, "Delight yourself in the LORD and He will give you the desires of your heart" (Psalm 37:4) Oh—this is good! Isn't it? The key to seizing the day is choosing life through being passionate about Him.

We can know if we're passionate about God. There is further instruction about loving the Lord our God. The Scriptures say, "...Now choose life, so that you and your children may live and that you may love the LORD your God, listen to his voice, and hold fast to him. For the LORD is your life..." (Deuteronomy 30:19-20). We know we have chosen life and are passionate about God when:

- **We listen to Him**. We're to "listen to His voice." We hear God speak to us through the conviction of God's Spirit, our self-coach. He leads us to feel uncomfortable about things that don't bring glory to God. Our listening to Him brings about something else.
- **We place our faith in Him**. We're to "hold fast to Him." He's the one who gives us value and we hold on to Him. We refuse to let go because we know the

alternative will just mess us up. We hold on to God because we can't "do this life" alone. What else?

- **We serve Him.** The Scripture teaches, "For the LORD is your life." I love this phrase! If this is true of me, then it means the Lord is the one who gives meaning to my life. He's the reason I live. He's the reason I get up every morning. We're not finished yet.

Those Who Choose Life Don't Compromise

God warns the people of Israel about compromise. He says, "But if your heart turns away and you are not obedient, and if you are drawn away to bow down to other gods and worship them, I declare to you this day that you will certainly be destroyed. You will not live long in the land you are crossing the Jordan to enter and possess" (Deuteronomy 30:17-18). Here's a Tim paraphrase: "Bad stuff happens when we compromise and begin loving someone more than we love God." Satan tempts us for a reason. He wants to influence us to lose our influence. If he succeeds, we spiritually fail. Again, it has everything to do with our desire. How does he do it? We discover the answers to the question as we learn information about those who choose death.

Those Who Choose Death Misuse Their Time

The more time we spend with God, the more we love God. The more time we spend away from God, the more we love what has kept us from spending time with God. Makes sense to me! Some say absence makes the heart grow fonder. In some cases — as we have relationships with other people — this is true. However, in many cases, absence makes the heart forget. This is certainly true in our relationship with God. We can't seize the day if our day doesn't include time spent with God. Our minds must be directed to Him, to remember Him so we will follow Him. There's a second way Satan draws our attention away from God.

Those Who Choose Death Prioritize Acceptance from Man Rather Than Acceptance from God

We're to love God first, not second or third or fourth or even tenth. Satan successfully leads us to compromise when God drops down the priority list. Those who do this are more concerned for their new god than the true God. We begin to live for the approval of this new god. We don't seize the day. We're living for the wrong purpose and "trouble's coming"! We don't choose life.

We have another choice:

The Choice: Manipulation or Investment

We seize the day when we influence correctly. The Scriptures teach, "Now choose life, so that you and your children may live" (Deuteronomy 30:19). Our decisions not only affect us, but they also affect those we lead—especially our children. Do you remember how we choose life? We choose life when we're passionate about God and when we don't compromise. If we're passionate about God, we influence by making an investment in others. If we compromise, we influence through manipulation. So a daily choice for us is manipulation or investment. Let's learn about each.

Those Who Choose Manipulation Use Their Influence to Control Others for Personal Gain

Their happiness comes from what they receive. They feast on what the world has to offer. Their motive is to gain as much as they can, and because of this, they use people and situations to improve their position. They have a "served" mindset. In other words, they believe everyone is here to serve them. If they're being served well, they're happy. If they aren't, their world breaks down and they begin to emotionally respond in harmful ways. How? They discourage others. They also lose their hope because their trust has been placed in something that doesn't truly satisfy.

Those Who Choose Investment Use Their Influence to Help People Succeed

Their happiness comes from the joy they experience. They're joyful because they're giving. Their motive is to help others improve and become successful, which leads them to give of their time, talents, and resources. They have a "serve" mindset. They're willing to reach out toward others with love to help bring about positive change. They're an investment agent, encouraging others.

What choices are you making daily? Are you choosing:

- Today or tomorrow?
- Risk or safety?
- Life or death?
- Investment or manipulation?

The Big Ending

Let's consider the first choice once again. Are you living for today or tomorrow? What will you do today to begin moving toward emotional health? It's time to look in the mirror and see the real you. Who do you trust in? Emotional success begins with proper faith placement. Are you ready to move forward by trusting in the One who can help you? You may be one of those people who've been waiting for tomorrow to give your life to God. You've been waiting for all of the stars to align perfectly before you accept what Jesus has done for you on the cross and through His resurrection. Let me help you understand when that occurs. The stars align when you know the following:

- I know God loves me.
- I know I've failed Him by doing things wrong and it bothers me because I know I've hurt Him.
- I know I need forgiveness for my sins because I want a relationship with Him and I know my failures are standing in the way.
- I know Jesus died for me on the cross to take the punishment I deserve for my failures in order to prove God's love for me.
- I know Jesus came back to life to defeat death once and for all to help me know He is the most powerful and that through Him I can overcome my problems.
- I know I need to accept what Jesus did for me and make Him Lord of my life.

If you believe these things, then you know what you need to know to place your faith in Jesus. A miracle has just happened. I know this because no one can convince you of these things other than God. Paul writes, "For it is by grace you have been saved, through faith—and this not from yourselves, it is the gift of God—not by works, so that no one can boast. For we are God's workmanship, created in Christ Jesus to do good works, which God prepared in advance for us to do" (Ephesians 2:8-10). We are saved when we know we are loved by God and are willing to place our faith in Him. He has proven He's trustworthy through His love. This faith really is the source of an "emotionally smart" life. It's the foundation for emotional success. I want to encourage you right now to accept Christ by faith through praying a prayer of commitment. Pray these words and mean them with your heart:

Dear God,
I know You love me. I know I have sinned against You. I need Your forgiveness. I know You sent Jesus to die on the cross to take my punishment for me. I know He was resurrected to give me life. I accept Jesus into my heart right now to be my Savior. I confess You, Jesus, as my Lord. Thank You for saving me. Help me to live a life of love as I continue to trust in you. Thank You for saving me. In Jesus' name I pray, Amen.

It's time for another choice. The choice is risk or safety. I want to encourage you to let others know about your decision to give your life to Christ. Be transparent! Be real! Satan wants you to fear what they will say about your decision. Take the risk! God wants you to find your strength in Him and to be obedient by letting people know about your relationship with Him. Sharing our faith with others confirms in our hearts what we've done. It's evidence we were serious about the decision we made to place our faith in Jesus.

If you prayed this prayer of commitment, I want to congratulate you on the most important decision you will ever make. This is one prayer God always says yes to. You have what you need to begin the journey toward emotional health. You've chosen life over death! Continue to trust in Him, let Him control your mind and heart, and allow God to use your emotions as an investment. I'm praying for you!

End Notes

Chapter Two

1. Department of Health and Human Services, "Anxiety Disorders" (Bethesda, Maryland: National Institute of Mental Health, 2006), 1-15.
2. Gerhart, Clark, *Say Goodbye to Stubborn Sin* (Lake Mary, FL: Siloam, 2005), 142.
3. Gerhart, 142.
4. Janet Maccaro, *Breaking the Grip of Dangerous Emotions* (Lake Mary, FL: Siloam, 2005), 109.
5. Ibid., 110.
6. Adele B. Lynn, *The EQ Difference: A Powerful Plan for Putting Emotional Intelligence to Work* (New York, NY: AMACOM, 2005), 38.
7. Ibid, 47.

Chapter Three

8. Daniel Goleman, *Emotional Intelligence: Why it can matter more than IQ* (New York: Bantam Books, 1995), 6.
9. Stoop, David, *You Are What You Think* (Grand Rapids, MI: Fleming H. Revell, 1996), 12.

10. Ibid., 12.
11. Ibid., 12.
12. Ibid., 12.
13. Ibid., 29.

Chapter Five

14. Bill Bryson, *A Short History of Nearly Everything* (New York, NY: Broadway Books, 2003), 20.
15. Kassian, Mary, *Conversation Peace* (Nashville, TN: LifeWay Press, 2001), 75.
16. Ibid., 75.
17. Max Lucado, *A Love Worth Giving* (Nashville, TN: W Publishing Group, 2002), 43, 44.
18. Ken Lottis, "On Religion: It Takes Courage to Admit You're Lost," *Mercer Island Reporter*, 12-12-2002.
19. Kassian, 83.

Chapter Six

20. Lucado, *A Love Worth Giving*, 46-47.
21. "Prisoner Sues God," Ananova.com, October 20, 2005, http://www.ananova.com/news/story/sm_1576068.html.
22. Tim LaHaye, Bob Phillips, *Anger is a Choice* (Grand Rapids, MI: Zondervan, 2002), 19-20.
23. David Augsburger, *Care Enough To Confront* (Ventura, CA: Regal Books, 1981), 37.
24. Ibid., 38.
25. Ibid., 38.
26. Ibid., 40.
27. "Angry Wife Gets Revenge Via Ebay," FoxNews.com, http://www.foxnews.com/story/0,2933,160390,00.html.
28. "50 Ways To Fix Your Life," *U.S. News & World Report*, (12-27-04 to 01-03-05), Vol. 137, no. 23; p. 86.

Chapter Seven

29. Thomas Lindberg, "Jealousy," *Leadership*, Vol. VI, No. 4, Fall 1985, 76.
30. Alain de Botton, *Status Anxiety* (New York, NY: Vintage Books, 2004), 27.

Chapter Eight

31. Webster's New World Dictionary, 32.
32. Stoop, 131.
33. Douglas Rumford, *Scared to Life* (Wheaton, IL: Victor Books, 1994), 21.
34. Maccaro, 11-12.
35. Goleman, 65.
36. Maccaro, 33.
37. Ibid., 35.
38. Ibid., 35.
39. Ibid., 39.
40. Ibid., 39.
41. Stoop, 132.

Chapter Nine

42. Mark Buchanan, *Your God Is Too Safe* (Sisters, OR: Multnomah, 2001), 47.
43. James S. Hirsch, *The Miraculous Journey of Rubin Carter* (Boston, MA: Houghton Muffin, 2000), 310.
44. Max Lucado, *The Applause of Heaven* (Nashville, TN: Word, 1996), 100.
45. Don Colbert, *Deadly Emotions* (Nashville, TN: Thomas Nelson Publishers, 2003), 127.
46. Les Parrott, Neil Clark Warren, *Love the Life You Live* (Wheaton, IL: Tyndale House Publishers, Inc., 2004), 54.

47. Ibid., 54.
48. Warren, Parrott, 65.
49. Lewis, C.S., *Reflections on the Psalms* (New York, NY: Harcourt, Brace and World, Inc, 1958), 254.

Chapter Ten

50. Don Colbert, *Stress Less* (Lake Mary, FL: Siloam, 2005), 57.
51. George, 44.
52. Randall Arthur, *Wisdom Hunter* (Sisters: OR: Multnomah Publishers, 1991), 211.
53. Karen S. Peterson, "Study Links Depression, Suicide Rates to Teen Sex," *USA Today*, 6-03-2003, Section D, 8.
54. J. P. Moreland, Laus Issler, *Lost Virtue of Happiness* (Colorado Springs, CO: NavPress, 2006), 21-22.
55. Ibid., 21-22.
56. Andrea Sachs, Juliet Schor, "Junk Culture," *Time Magazine*, October, 2004.
57. Sora Song, "Do Heartfelt Prayers Help the Heart?" *Time Magazine*, Thursday, March 30, 2006.
58. Ibid.

Chapter Eleven

59. Charlotte Davis Kasl, *Finding Joy: 101 Ways to Free Your Spirit and Dance with Life* (New York, NY: HarperPerennial, 1994), xvi.
60. Ibid., vxii.
61. Chris Heath, "Unbearable Bradness of Being," *Rolling Stone Magazine*, 10-28-99., Vol. 1, Issue 824, 66-74. http://jmm.aaa.net.au/articles/2242.htm.
62. Marilyn Elias, "Psychologists Now Know What Makes People Happy," *USA Today*, 12-09-2002, Section A, 1.

63. Osho, *Joy: The Happiness That Comes from Within* (New York, NY: St. Martin's Griffin, 2004), vii.
64. Ibid., vii.
65. Ibid., 7.
66. Johnson, Robert A., *Ecstasy: Understanding the Psychology of Joy* (San Francisco, CA: Harper San Francisco, 1987), vi-vii.
67. Johnson, 22.
68. Ruth A. Tucker, "Ministries of Mercy: Mother Teresa," *Christian History*, Issue 65, Vol. 19, No.1), 22. Internet Site - http://ctlibrary.com/4397.
69. Osho, 9-10.
70. Erik J. Giltay, **"Dispositional Optimism and All-Cause and Cardiovascular Mortality in a Prospective Cohort of Elderly Dutch Men and Women,"** Archives of General Psychiatry, November, 2004; Vol. 61, 1126-1135.
71. Jill Lieber, "Teen Riding Wave of Amazing Grace," USA Today, March 19, 2004, Section C, 15.

Chapter Twelve

72. Erwin McManus, *Seizing Your Divine Moment* (Nashville, TN: Thomas Nelson Publishers, 2002), 23.
73. Ibid., 52.
74. John Piper, *Don't Waste Your Life* (Wheaton, IL: Crossway Books, 2003), 87.
75. Ibid., 87.
76. McManus, 47-48.

Printed in the United States
214010BV00006B/3/P

9 780981 509525